Doodlebugs and Rockets
Norfolk and Suffolk
1944–1945

Cut-away drawing of V1 produced by British Air Intelligence in September 1944. The spheres contain compressed air for the guidance systems and to pressurise the fuel supply.

Doodlebugs and Rockets
Norfolk and Suffolk
1944–1945

John F Bridges

POPPYLAND
PUBLISHING

Copyright © John F Bridges.
This edition 2023 published by Poppyland Publishing, Lowestoft, NR32 3BB.

www.poppyland.co.uk

ISBN 978 1 869831 11 0

Designed and typeset in 10.5 on 13.5 pt Gilgamesh Pro.

Printed by Severn, Gloucester.

Picture credits:

Author's collection, 13, 34, 35 (top), 39, 40 (bottom), 45, 47, 59, 60, 62, 91 (right), 104, 105 (top), 115 (top)
Bentwaters Cold War Museum, 28
Bowles, Andy, 66, 68
Collis, Bob, 41, 95, 97 (middle & bottom), 98, 109 (bottom), 116
Framlingham Historical Archive, 81
Hadleigh Archive, 65
Imperial War Museum (IWM), 21, 23, 44 (bottom), 52, 53, 54, 55, 75, 76
Jennings, Mike, RAF Coltishall, 24, 25, 40 (top)
Kindred, David, 91 (left), 97 (top), 105 (bottom)
Mitchell, Bruce, 38
National Archives Washington DC, 18, 20, 30, 32, 35 (bottom), 94, 107
Norfolk Record Office, PD 78/152, 85
Parham Airfield Museum, ii, 93
Power Of The Past Collection, 10
Smith, Eileen, 82, 83
Smith, John, Felixstowe at War, 44, 67 (bottom), 74, 77, 80, 86, 89, 102
Snelling, Steve, 15, 84, 109 (top), 112 (top), 115 (bottom)
Suffolk Archives, A1608/1, 96
The National Archives, HO 198/103, 110, 112 (bottom)
Wood, Derek, Attack Warning Red, 67 (top)

Front Cover: Painting by Lindsay Huggins of a V1 over Parham airfield, with tracer fire from Bofors guns on the coast and searchlights. Based on original photo on page 93.

Contents

Acknowledgements

Many people have kindly helped me with this project and I would like to thank them for their memories, guidance, technical expertise and assistance with material. Without them this book would not have made it into print.

Steve Snelling is a Norfolk author who has produced countless articles and many books relating to wartime activities. I was therefore delighted when he agreed to provide the Foreword. Thank you Steve.

Since starting on this work some five years ago, I soon became aware of the researches of aviation historian Bob Collis of Lowestoft. Bob kindly agreed to not only review the text but has made available pictures and details from his own extensive archives on the subject. Thanks Bob.

David Sims, co-author of *A Very Dangerous Locality, The landscape of the Suffolk Sandlings in the Second World War*, has greatly assisted me through his knowledge and sources on The Diver Strip. David Heath and Jim Rudkin of the Bawdsey Radar Trust have helped me with the complexities of radar, while Andy Bowles has shared his great knowledge of the Royal Observer Corps. My thanks to you all.

There is limited information on Operations Aphrodite and Anvil. I have relied heavily on Jack Olsen's book *Aphrodite, Desperate Mission*, published in 1970. Lt Col Roy Forrest was in charge of Operation Aphrodite in 1944 and stated "…the author tells the story of Aphrodite exactly as it happened". I am most thankful to Evan and Gregg Olsen for allowing me to reference the book.

Staff at the Norfolk Record Office, Suffolk Archives and The National Archives in Kew have all been most helpful in my search for original material. A big thank you to everyone for their assistance.

I would also like to thank the many people who have also helped in one way or another and to anyone I may have inadvertently forgotten.

Ethel Ayers, Louisa Beattie, Jane Bloom, Adrian Barrell, Ray Beales, Alan Beevis, David Chaplin, Frank Chaplin, Mary Cracknell, Margaret Cutting, Robert Dalby, Alan Davies, Bill Flemming, Alison and Simon Garrett, Simon Gladas, Pearl Goodall, Ann Hammond, Douglas Harper, Gerald Hawes, Karen Haynes, Hattie Hearn, Jerry Hill, Bob Hoggar, Lindsay Huggins, Michael Jillings, Bill Kemble, Roger Kennell, Caroline Lugo, Bernard Mills, Bruce Mitchell, Margaret Moore, Mick Muttitt, John Norman, Brian Page, John Pridige, Frank Rowe, Russell Ruffles, Peter Senior, Eileen Smith, Jennie Smith, Gordon Stannard, Danny Staff, Stephen Sullivan, Michael Usher, Peter Watkins, Lydia Wilkins, Roger Wilson, Ken Wright,

Stuart Yeomans.

Thanks also to my sister Annie for checking the text for grammatical horrors and to my wife Pat for all the look-ups, her knowledge of parishes and putting up with all the time I spent on this project.

And finally, a special thanks to Poppyland Publishing for taking on my work and seeing it through to publication.

All reasonable efforts have been made to locate owners of copyright material and any requests for corrections in this respect should be directed to the author via Poppyland Publishing.

John F Bridges, 2023.

Foreword

Some years ago I met a woman with a remarkable story to tell. In a field near a small village on the south-eastern outskirts of Norwich she recalled as a young girl witnessing the dramatic crash-landing of an American bomber close to her home. It was a story of courage and sacrifice tinged with tragedy that had made a lasting impression. In the course of our conversation, almost as an aside, she mentioned another wartime incident, one that was so terrible and so terrifying as to make her sense of shock still seem palpable more than 60 years later.

She remembered how she had been playing with a group of children on the edge of Bramerton when the peace of an early autumn evening was suddenly shattered by an explosion that came quite literally out of the blue. The force of the blast was enough to hurl two brothers 12 feet across their back yard and to strip the clothes off another hapless youngster as she made her way home along a nearby country lane. Though they didn't know it then, they were part of a growing number of people across East Anglia who found themselves at the receiving end of one of the Second World War's most secret and most sophisticated weapons—the V2 rocket.

The story of that most improbable of terror campaigns, the first in history to be waged by ballistic missiles, forms a key part of John Bridges' ground-breaking new study which seeks to put into context the myriad of deliberate and haphazard attacks that menaced the civilian populations of Norfolk and Suffolk along with the thousands of Allied servicemen and women based there during the last year of the war. Beginning with the assault by V1s, the so-called pilotless 'flying bombs', he chronicles the progress of an aerial offensive like no other which culminated by geographical mischance in a mercifully misdirected attempt to wreak havoc on the people of Norwich and Ipswich by V2 rockets.

In what amounts to the most detailed examination of the air assault yet produced, he pinpoints the often random fall of the missiles, assesses the damage wrought by them and the defences that they spawned as well as the counter-measures employed (not always successfully) in an attempt to combat the threat. Intertwined with the impressive array of statistical data are the personal recollections of mostly ordinary people, many of them no more than children at the time, who were caught up in one of the lesser-known 'blitzes' of the war.

At a time when Russian missiles continue to rain death and destruction on the people of Ukraine, their stories serve as vivid reminders of the terrible toll so nearly inflicted close to home by an aerial bombardment that diverted resources, frayed nerves and strained credulity but ultimately proved an abject failure.

Steve Snelling

V2 at launch site in wooded area, surrounded by support vehicles. An Allied test firing near Cuxhaven in October 1945.

Introduction

By 1944, the Second World War was in its fifth year, and following the D-Day invasion of Normandy there was hope that there would eventually be a successful outcome. But only seven days later the country was under attack from a new form of warfare, the Vengeance-Weapon V1. This was an aircraft with an explosive warhead, but no pilot. They were aimed at London and soon earned the name 'doodlebug'. In the first phase of these attacks they were ramp launched from France, but several lost their way and ended up in Suffolk.

It was the second phase that would have consequences for Norfolk and Suffolk because they were now being launched from aircraft over the North Sea and making their way overland to London. Our fighter planes, along with the artillery now in place on the coast, would create a formidable defence against them. There would, however, be many local incidents when damaged doodlebugs caused destruction, injury and loss of life.

A further type of Vengeance Weapon, the V2 rocket, would soon be unleashed. The concept of rockets for space travel has been with us for a long time now, but their accelerated development in the war was for belligerent purposes against this country, culminating in the first attacks in September 1944. Several of the early ones were targeted on Norwich. The rockets were expensive, complicated and made at enormous human cost by slave labour. They were unreliable and inaccurate, with many exploding in rural areas of Norfolk and Suffolk. In London, it was a different matter.

My interest in this subject started while gathering information for *A Suffolk Town in Wartime, Framlingham 1939 to 1945*. My father was a Special Constable, and a story handed down was that he heard a doodlebug coming over the town, followed by the motor cutting out and, after a period of silence, a large explosion. This was the V1 that impacted near Framlingham Hall at midday on 19 July 1944 causing damage to property, but fortunately no casualties.

Ethel Smith was 13 years old at the time and a pupil at Mills Grammar School. They had been warned about the doodlebugs and told that there was a ten-second period between the motor cutting out and the explosion. On hearing the V1 they all dived under their desks as instructed. The motor then cut out and soon after they heard the explosion. The girls then emerged from under their desks and carried on with the lesson.

The Second World War is a vast subject and the V-weapons are a very important part of it. There are many books which have detailed information on them and a select bibliography is included for those seeking the full story. The main aim of this

11

book is to provide a local history record of the V1 and V2 incidents that impacted Norfolk and Suffolk, along with some commentary on those events. Appendices I to IV list all incidents. References are provided in the text, mainly for matters of local interest.

Both counties played an important role in combating these new terror weapons by means of countless missions from the many airfields, the development of Radar, the Anti-Aircraft guns of the Diver Strip, the Royal Observer Corps, and all the men and women who were involved. It has only been possible to highlight certain aspects of these roles as each one would merit a book on its own.

The V-weapons or Vengeance Weapons (Vergeltungswaffen) soon gained their own names:

V1. FZG 76. The 'flying bomb' was powered by a pulse-jet engine. Common names for it were 'diver', 'doodlebug', 'buzz-bomb', 'fly', 'robot' and PAC (pilotless aircraft).

V2. The A4. This was a true rocket with names such as 'Big Ben', 'Long Range Rocket' (LRR) and 'Flying Pencil'. I will endeavour to use just V1 and V2 except when quoting from documents.

The V-weapon attacks against this country covered a period from 13 June 1944 to 29 March 1945. In that time official figures, excluding military personnel, show that 8,938 civilians were killed and 24,504 were seriously wounded by these weapons. See Appendix V for general statistics.

There were 106 V1 and 42 V2 incidents in Norfolk and Suffolk along with a great number that blew up or were destroyed off the coast. Yet common understanding is that they were aimed at the obvious and suitably large target of London. So why were so many ending up such a long way from their intended target? This started a long and interesting journey into a period of time that is almost lost to memory. Anyone who is at least 80 years of age might recall such incidents as a young child or teenager and I have been fortunate that several people have provided me with their first-hand experiences.

The Vengeance Weapons

Although the V1 was the first of these weapons to be launched against England, the V2 rocket programme had been under development for a longer period of time.

The V1

The Luftwaffe was developing a pilotless aircraft with an explosive warhead on the north peninsula of Peenemunde, located on the Baltic Sea island of Usedom. Early proposals were not considered acceptable to the Air Ministry and further work continued, now in conjunction with the Fieseler aircraft company and Argus Motoren, who developed the pulse-jet engine. The V1 was a smaller and simpler device than the complicated and expensive V2.

The overall V1 length was just over 27 feet with a wing span of around 16 feet. It weighed about two tons, with the warhead just under a ton, of which the explosive contributed over 3/4 ton. The in-flight speed varied, but was typically between 300 and 400 mph with an initial range up to 160 miles although later versions could exceed that. Various sources show differences in the data for both V1 and V2, the above being typical values.

The pulse jet is a device whereby air is forced into a chamber through a set of vanes. Low-grade petrol from a 150-gallon tank is sprayed into the chamber, which is ignited by a sparking plug to create the initial explosion. The pressure closes the inlet vanes and the expanding gases are forced out through a tail pipe and provide the thrust. The subsequent drop in pressure in the combustion chamber then opens the inlet vanes again and the whole cycle is repeated.

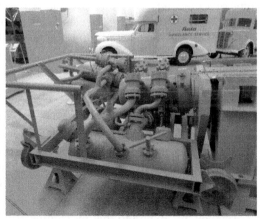

The V1 was located on a trolley on the launch ramp. Compressed air and electrical connections were made to the motor from an external unit and the combustion process started. To launch the weapon it was necessary for it to reach a speed of approximately 250 mph to continue the ram-air process. The Walter steam catapult combined T-Stoff (hydrogen

High-pressure steam from the Walter generator trolley propelled the V1 to a launch speed of around 250 mph. Generator seen here coupled to launch ramp on right. IWM Duxford.

13

peroxide) with Z-Stoff (sodium permanganate) to produce high-pressure steam which was fed into the cylinder along the length of the ramp. A piston within the cylinder was connected to the V1 and powered the launch. The piston and trolley then fell away to the ground and were reused.

The identification from aerial photographs of what would be known as 'ski sites' (the long storage buildings had a curved end, resembling a ski) provided the first indications of where the weapons were stored and would be launched from. By the end of 1943, 88 of these sites had been detected with another 50 suspected. They were heavily bombed by the Allies, which led to the development of 'modified sites' that were well camouflaged and very difficult to locate and destroy. By early June 1944, 66 of these new sites had been found, many in the Somme—Pas de Calais region.

The V1 was aimed at its target, with three gyroscopes providing corrections via servo motors to the elevators in order to maintain the course. These were powered by compressed air from two wire-bound-spherical containers. At a predetermined time after launch, detonators were fired which locked the rudder and elevators. Two spoilers were extended to put the missile into a steep dive. The intention was for the V1 to power dive to the ground, local examples were at Bealings on 18 August and Stratford St Andrew on 12 October. In the report for Maryon Road in Ipswich on 1 September, there is conflicting information where one person stated that it power dived into the ground while another said the motor cut out. A survey of some 200 incidents showed that only 4 per cent of them did make a powered dive.

In most cases the detonators caused the fuel supply to stop and are the reason for the period of silence before the explosion. The actual period could vary considerably. The report for the Carlton Colville incident on 19 November gave a time of 45 seconds, and some are reported to have been even longer. A period of 10—15 seconds is more typical. The silence following the fuel cut-off was terrifying for those on the receiving end, leaving them little time to find shelter and with the sure knowledge that devastation was about to occur. The explosion caused much blast damage although crater size could be relatively small, particularly when the V1 landed at a shallow angle.

V1s would also be launched from aircraft as that was part of the flying-bomb directive ordered in May 1944. However, the practical implications of carrying such a weapon under one wing meant its accuracy was even further compromised. They were launched from Heinkel He 111 aircraft operated by III/KG 3 from three airfields located to the north of Paris. After some early launches, the first clearly defined period of air-launched attacks started on 9/10 July. The Allied advances in Normandy put an end to that by 15 July. III/KG 3 then moved to two airfields in Holland where raids started on 18/19 July. After only seven weeks, they again had to move, this time into north-west Germany.

As the ramp-launched sites had been overrun, this meant air launching was the only method now available and the size of the operation was to be expanded. KG 53 had been on the Eastern Front and was brought back to be trained for air launches. III/KG 3 was then merged with KG 53 from 15 October, operating from nine airfields. It was the lack of fuel for the planes that eventually spelt the end of air launches, the last in Suffolk being on 13 January 1945 when one landed at Capel St Andrew.

There was a final hurrah when Phase 3 commenced with modified ramp-launched V1s fired from Holland on 3 March 1945. They would need to have an extended range, and evidence of this was found in February when a crashed one was recovered in Belgium. This final phase was short lived, with the last one being shot down off Orfordness on 29 March 1945.

THE V2

The first experiments with rockets were carried out many centuries ago and scientists had long been devising ways of extending their range. It was in 1930 that the German Army Weapons Office invited Captain Walter Dornberger to set up a team for investigating the means of mass producing rockets for military purposes. Two years later, the new facility at Kummersdorf, south of Berlin, was ready to start experiments. The leader of the team was a man whose name would become synonymous with rockets for many years into the future – Wernher von Braun. The first rocket, Aggregate 1 (A1), was very small and did not prove successful. The A2 had more success and by the end of 1934 had reached a height of more

Mock up of V2 rocket at Peenemunde. It was brought to the launch location on a Meiller trailer.

than 10,000 feet.

Further developments led to the conclusion that Kummersdorf was no longer suitable as a location for firing rockets, due to security issues and its proximity to Berlin. The Baltic island of Usedom was selected as the new site and specifically the Peenemunde peninsula, another name that would endure long after the war. The next rocket was the A3, but facilities were not ready at Peenemunde. Testing took place on another island but poor weather conditions led to several failures and the A3 programme was abandoned, leading on to the A4.

The Reich's Ministry of Aviation purchased the north peninsula of Usedom in 1936, with the cost being shared between the Army (Heer) and the Air Force (Luftwaffe). From 1938, the army would develop the V2 on the east of Peenemunde, while the Luftwaffe progressed the V1 to the north and west of the peninsula. Despite the rocket programme having been established for some time, it would be the V1 that was first fired in anger against England.

The Peenemunde facility was a vast complex of around 700 buildings which were dominated by the 30 MW power station. Much of the output supplied electrical power for the refrigeration plant to produce the liquid oxygen for the rockets. In addition, there were research, production and test facilities, along with workshops, office blocks and living quarters. From 1943, the manpower for these facilities was housed in labour camps and the concentration camp at Trassenheide. The conditions for these people were horrendous and over the war years many more died under these inhumane conditions than were ever killed by the weapons they were forced to produce.

Hitler had been diverting large sums of money into the construction of conventional weapons of warfare, and although interested in the rocket programme he was not prepared to provide the necessary funding as there was insufficient evidence regarding its potential success. Work continued under these constraints on the A4, and a smaller version, the A5. After Britain declared war on Germany in September 1939, von Braun still had nothing that could contribute in a practical way, so the project remained short of funding.

The rapid advance of German forces in the early days of the war saw funding cut again as such untried and expensive weapons were not considered necessary if the war was to be quickly won. However, failing to gain air supremacy over Britain would see funding reinstated. Work on the A4 proceeded apace, and in October 1942 the first successful launch saw the rocket exceeding 3,000 mph and a height of nearly 60 miles. Later that year, Hitler signed the order to commence mass production, but it was not given any special priority and it would be nearly two years before the first V2 would reach English soil.

In May 1943, the V1 and V2 were demonstrated to the upper echelons of the

Reich. The V2s successfully launched but the V1s did not. The Allied raids on Hamburg on 24 July enraged Hitler and he demanded retaliation. He was shown films of the successful launch of the V2 and agreed to provide all the money and labour needed to develop both weapons.

The V2 was 46 feet long with a body diameter of about 5 ½ feet. At launch, with warhead, water, ethyl alcohol, and liquid oxygen, it weighed nearly 13 tons. The explosive in the warhead itself was nearly 3/4 ton. The rocket engine could produce 55,000 to 66,000 lb of thrust for 65 seconds enabling it to reach a maximum speed of about 3,600 mph, falling to below 2,500 mph near impact. It reached a height of 50 to 60 miles giving it a range of 200 to 220 miles. The V2 was nearly twice as long, and more than six times heavier than the V1.

'The Vulture' of the 390th Bomb Group at Parham, with ground crew, was just one of 722 Flying Fortresses and Liberators that took part in the raid on V1 'ski sites' on 24 December 1943.

Attacking the Launch Sites

The V-Weapon campaign against Britain started with the first V1s on 13 June 1944 and ended when the last one was shot down off Orfordness on 29 March 1945. The V2 assaults started on 8 September 1944 and ended on 27 March 1945 when the last one exploded at Orpington in Kent. Very little was initially known about these secret weapons, and intelligence needed to be gathered to formulate plans for bombing the sites.

In September 1939 a Special Flight was formed under Fighter Command to carry out aerial reconnaissance over enemy territory. The guns of the Supermarine Spitfire, along with its radio and non-essential equipment, were removed, relying on its high speed to avoid enemy aircraft. When the photographic images were viewed in three dimensions, the details on the ground became readily apparent. The large increase in personnel required to interpret the photos for all three services saw their relocation from London to Medmenham in Buckinghamshire. The aircraft were formed into the Photographic Reconnaissance Unit (PRU).

It was not until 1943 that it was possible for the PRU's attention to be focused on activities at Peenemunde, where information suggested some form of testing might be taking place, and also anywhere along the French coast within about 130 miles of London, a vast area. The diligence of the interpreters combined with the photographic material obtained at great risk did lead to the identification of rocket–like structures at Peenemunde. Models were constructed to aid understanding of what was taking place there. It was soon established that action was needed to halt the construction of these facilities.

The first serious reports of the sighting of what appeared to be a new weapon were in April 1943, although there were earlier observations of what may have been rockets. The son-in-law of Winston Churchill, the MP Duncan Sandys, was appointed chairman of the Committee for Flying Bomb Counter-Measures which would be called Bodyline. Since there was no conclusive proof, further information was sought from foreign agents, prisoners of war and aerial reconnaissance. By the end of June he was able to prepare a report containing information on the rocket.

Bomber Command had many priorities but on the night of 17 August, Operation Hydra despatched nearly 600 mostly Lancaster and Halifax heavy bombers, along with Mosquitoes, in three waves to Peenemunde. There was much loss of life on the ground, many were Germans but a greater number were in the labour camps. The third wave of the raid was heavily hit by night fighters and the overall RAF losses amounted to 40 aircraft, 245 killed and 145 taken prisoner. The raid set back rocket production, possibly by five to six weeks, and led to the majority of V2

Bomb damage to a V1 launch ramp in the Pas de Calais region.

development being moved to Poland. The V1 area at Peenemunde had not been attacked, but the loss of slave labour had a major impact there also.

By the end of the war there were 72 active airfields in Norfolk and Suffolk, from where many missions were flown to attack the V-weapon sites and the infrastructure that supplied them.[1] The USAAF bases were in the majority, and on 27 August they carried out their first attack on the mighty block house at Watten. The second element of this force consisted of 65 Flying Fortresses made up entirely from Bomb Groups based in Norfolk and Suffolk: 94th (Bury St Edmunds), 95th (Horham), 96th (Snetterton Heath), 100th (Thorpe Abbotts), 385th (Great Ashfield), 388th (Knettishall) and 390th (Framlingham).[2]

Operation Crossbow, which commenced in August 1943, was the codename for attacks by both British and American forces, called 'Noball' missions. On Christmas Eve, the largest Allied force assembled so far included 722 Fortresses and Liberators along with 541 P-47 and P-51 fighters, plus 221 B-26 medium bombers. The RAF sent 48 medium bombers and 456 Spitfires.[3] Of the 23 target sites, only three were completely destroyed, highlighting the difficulties associated with them. Although the 'ski sites' were readily identified by the shape of some of the buildings, as a target they were small and consequently difficult to bomb accurately. These missions were often conducted when bad weather prevented more distant raids into Germany. The early missions were sometimes thought of

Halifax on bombing raid over Mimoyecques 'heavy site'. This was later found to be the location of the V3 long-range gun. © IWM, CH4458.

as 'milk runs', but that all changed when flak significantly increased and they were forced to fly much higher.

There was much disagreement between senior members of both air forces and politicians regarding the policies behind Crossbow. It was viewed by the military as a distraction from the main work of neutralising enemy installations, particularly in the run up to the D-Day invasion in June 1944. It was not until then that a new relentless campaign started which would continue towards the end of August. These raids were mainly conducted with Lancaster, Halifax and Mosquito bombers, and a smaller number with Stirlings.

No. 635 Squadron operated Lancasters out of Downham Market. On 4 August they went on a daylight mission to mark and bomb a V1 storage depot at Trossy St Maxim in northern France. The plane of Acting Squadron Leader Ian Bazalgette DFC was hit by heavy flak when approaching the target. He was able to keep control marking and bombing the target, but eventually had to order the crew to bail out before attempting to land in a field. The plane exploded, killing two of the crew and Bazalgette. A year later he was posthumously awarded the Victoria Cross for his courage and devotion to duty.[4]

Allied forces conducted their attacks on many V-site installations in France, although for the very large sites, it was not clear for what purpose they had been built. The Germans had considered two main options for deployment of both the V1 and V2, either from large, heavily constructed buildings or from several smaller mobile sites. Hitler had been in favour of the former, which led to the construction of the 'heavy sites' such as Watten, Wizernes and Mimoyecques in northern France. These were more visible to reconnaissance and therefore attracted much heavy bombing.

There were concerns that the preparations for D-Day would be affected by the start of the V1 campaign, but it took several days before the Germans were able to make their first launches towards England and by then eight of these sites had already been overrun. The first V1s were fired on 13 June, but of those launched; only four reached England. It was the second one which impacted at Bethnal Green in London that caused the first fatalities of the V-weapon campaign when six people were killed.

The attacks on 'ski sites' had dictated a move to smaller, well-concealed locations from late February 1944. These 'modified sites', often hidden amongst farm buildings, only became noticeable to air reconnaissance when the ramp was finally erected, and this would be camouflaged except when in use.

The USAAF 390th Heavy Bombardment Group based at Framlingham (Parham) was one of many Groups in Norfolk and Suffolk to carry out extensive raids on V-weapon sites. From August 1943 to July 1944, the 390th Bomb Group conducted 15 missions to the 'Rocket Coast', with the following examples. They show the uncertainty of the purpose of the sites.[5] Mimoyecques would turn out to be the location of Hitler's V3 supergun, which would have the potential to fire shells directly at London.

> Watten, 27 August 1943. The Group was only able to put up seven Fortresses to attack the target which was identified as an 'aeronautical installation', the exact purpose being unknown then.

> Quoeux, 24 December 1943. The 'pilotless aircraft site' was attacked by 36 planes.

> Mimoyecques, 19 March 1944. Around 21 planes sent to bomb the site.

> La Glacerie, 27 April 1944. Despite heavy flak, 21 planes dropped bombs with very good results.

> Fressin-Crepy, 6 July 1944. Last mission by Group on V-sites. There was good weather and no flak when 21 planes bombed the site.

The US fighter groups were heavily involved with attacks on the railways, which apart from the general movement of troops and munitions, were also essential for the transportation of V-weapons to the launch areas. On 2 August 1944, P-51D Mustangs of the 364th Group from Honington in Norfolk attacked camouflaged wagons in a siding. After initial assaults in line with the track, four planes then

Barnes Wallis designed the 1,200 lb Tallboy bomb. Having a terminal speed of up to 750 mph; it was able to collapse the foundations of buildings. © IWM, CH15367.

came in at right angles firing at the wagons. As the last plane fired, there was an enormous explosion which caused the loss of that plane; the other three were flipped over but fortunately recovered. The wagons contained V1 warheads and the only evidence of where they had been was a series of craters 30 feet wide and 10 feet deep.[6]

The 'heavy sites' proved resistant to conventional bombing. It was the introduction of Barnes Wallis's Tallboy bombs carried by Lancaster bombers that would make the difference. The second Tallboy raid to Watten on 25 July led to the abandonment of this site. Each bomb weighed 12,000 lb and could reach a speed of 750 mph when dropped from a height of 18,000 feet. Much of the destruction arose from structural collapse within the buildings, which was not evident from subsequent aerial reconnaissance. Although we now know these sites had mainly been abandoned, the Germans kept a token presence there to suggest they were active. Concerns remained that these massive structures were still a threat

Although the Crossbow campaign provided a concerted attack on the sites, V1s were launched in considerable numbers. In June, the first month of the V1 strikes in England, there were 1,435; in July it peaked to 2,435 before falling back to 1,450 in August, by which time the sites were being overrun by advancing Allied troops. Without Operation Crossbow these numbers would have been much greater and the strikes would have started earlier. The first V2 had not been launched at this time.

That would land in England on 8 September 1944, killing eight people with a further 20 being injured. Having a terminal speed of up to 2,500 mph it could not be shot down, although schemes were proposed to do just that. The only practical option was to destroy the V2s on their launch pads but that was going to be difficult as they were all fired from mobile platforms that were quickly hidden away. Intelligence came from many sources to try and identify these sites, most of which were located in Holland.

Attacks on the V2 sites and transport connections were carried out by Fighter Command, while the 2nd Tactical Air Force based on the continent was able to conduct large numbers of missions against transport targets. RAF Coltishall in Norfolk played a major role in what would become known as Operation Big Ben. Patrols were started in September 1944 with Mk IX Spitfires attacking transports and infrastructure with cannons and machine guns. From early December they were able to refuel at bases in Belgium, which enabled the clipped-wing Mk XVI to deliver one 500 lb bomb and two 250 lb bombs in a true dive-bomber role.[7]

Their targets were mainly determined from photo reconnaissance data which showed that most launch locations were hidden in wooded areas. The concern was always to select targets that minimised risk to the Dutch population. Precision raids were carried out on specific urban targets such as the one on 24 December against a block of flats being used to house V2 launch-troops.[8]

Matlaske was a satellite airfield of Coltishall but was subject to poor drainage. Spitfires were based there to combat the V2 menace, one of which had exploded very close to Coltishall on 29 September. However, by April 1945 Matlaske had been abandoned due to the water issues. 602 Squadron had already moved to Coltishall's other satellite airfield, Ludham, in February.[9]

Spitfires from RAF Coltishall were used in dive-bomber attacks on V2 sites. The planes were refuelled in Belgium, this allowed the Mk XV1 to carry one 500 lb and two 250 lb bombs.

The ability to increase the rate of firing V2s was limited by the supply of missiles and liquid oxygen. Spitfires kept up a relentless attack on the railway system, the launch sites and associated infrastructure buildings. There was now little in the way of Luftwaffe activity, with flak being the main concern, along with poor weather and mechanical problems with the aircraft. While patrolling the target areas it was common to see the contrail from a V2 launch, when its distance and directions were reported.

Flt Lt Raymond Baxter (second left) with pilots of 602 (City of Glasgow) Squadron, RAF Coltishall. They carried out many strikes on V2 sites and their associated infrastructure.

Flt Lt Raymond Baxter of 602 (City of Glasgow) Squadron led a flight of Spitfire XV1s against a target in a wooded area near The Hague on 14 February 1945. After pressing home their attacks they were suddenly confronted by a V2 rising off its launch pad. Flt Sgt 'Cupid' Love took aim and fired his cannons. Fortunately he did not hit any vital components otherwise they would not have survived to tell the tale.[10] Baxter in later years would be a familiar face on television, fronting programmes such as *Tomorrow's World*.

The priority in the attacks on V2 sites was to avoid collateral damage as many of the launch targets were close to residential areas in and around The Hague. One particular location which received regular attention was Haagsche-Bosch, a large wooded area which had been bombed for many weeks. There was an agreement that only fighter bombers would be used for such attacks and not medium/heavy bombers due to their poorer accuracy. However, the situation changed in February, allowing the 2nd Tactical Air Force to carry out such attacks when it had aircraft to spare.

On the morning of 3 March 1945, medium bombers (Bostons and Mitchells) carried out a raid on Haagsche-Bosch. The 56 aircraft involved dropped 96 tons of bombs.[11] A combination of errors led to the bombs landing on residential areas. The loss of life was 535 with 3,300 homes destroyed. This was a bitter blow to the pilots from Coltishall, who in their low-level raids had avoided such tragedy. No further attacks were made by medium bombers.

The last V2 launched against England landed at Orpington in Kent on 27 March 1945. The nature of the V2 launches from camouflaged locations near residential areas meant that precise attacks were needed on the sites and the infrastructure supplying them. Operation Big Ben had successfully pressed home these attacks and ostensibly reduced the number of V2 launches against this country.[12] The Spitfires from 12 Group operating from bases in East Anglia bore the brunt of these attacks.[13]

Notes

1. Norfolk & Suffolk Aviation Museum.
2. *www.iwm.org.uk*, ref. V111 Bomber Command 87.
3. Zaloga, S., *Operation Crossbow, 1944*, Osprey Publishing, 2018, p. 32.
4. Smith, G., *Norfolk Airfields in the Second World War*, Countryside Books, 1997, p. 89.
5. The Men and Officers of The 390th Bombardment Group, *The Story of The 390th Bombardment Group (H)*, 1947, p. 77.
6. Freeman, R., *The Mighty Eighth, a History of the US Army Air Force*, Macdonald and Jane's, 1978, p. 185.
7. Jennings, M., *Royal Air Force Coltishall*, Old Forge Publishing, 2007, p.130.
8. Ibid.
9. Ibid., p. 271.
10. Ibid., p. 134.
11. Grehan, J., *Hitler's V-Weapons, An Official History*, Frontline Books, 2020, p.183.
12. Cabell, C. and Thomas, G., *Operation Big Ben, 1944–1945*, Spellmount, 2004, p.103.
13. Ibid. 6, p. 130.

Operations Aphrodite and Anvil

Since the first V1s had landed, the bombing of targets connected with V2 rockets up to the middle of July 1944 was confined to four of the large sites, Mimoyecques, Watten, Siracourt and Wizernes. On 10 July, the bombing of these sites was halted except for certain special projects that were carried out by American forces.[1] Some intelligence reports suggested that very long-range rockets were being developed. The A9/10 was a two-stage rocket conceived in 1940 with an expected range up to 3,400 miles.[2] The potential for such long-range rockets led to concerns that they might be able to reach North America.

The USAAF developed an alternative strategy, code name Operation Aphrodite, with the naval equivalent Operation Anvil, to combat the rocket threat. The concept was to use war-weary bombers, strip them of all armament and unnecessary equipment and then pack the plane with explosives. The plane (drone) would take off with a pilot and an auto-pilot, who after setting the controls and arming the explosives would exit by parachute. A following plane (the mother ship) would then guide the drone by remote control, keeping it in sight and sending it onto the target. That was the theory. These were bold and dangerous missions setting off in the skies over Norfolk and Suffolk, with the population below blissfully unaware of what was going on.

Major General Doolittle approved the plan on 26 June 1944 with the assignment being given to the 562nd Bomb Squadron at RAF Honington. Ten war-weary B-17s were flown there to be stripped of all unnecessary equipment, including gun turrets and everything bar the pilot's seat. A detachment of the 3rd Bomb Division started to arrived at RAF Woodbridge (Sutton Heath) from 7 July with around 180 personnel, 14 'Special Fortresses', 2 Liberators and 8 Thunderbolts.[3] The base log noted, 'The Americans were carrying out a special mission and wished to use the runway at Woodbridge for the take off.'

RAF Woodbridge was no ordinary airfield but one constructed in 1943 specifically as an emergency 'crash-drome'. There was only one runway, 3,000 yards long (plus 1,500 yards extra for over/undershoots). The 250-yard wide runway was divided into three lanes; Amber for badly damaged and wheels-up landings, a central White lane for less damaged aircraft, and a Green lane for those low on fuel.[4]

The B-24 Liberator mother ship would need to have visual contact at all times so the upper wings of each drone were painted hi-vis yellow, and smoke pots attached to the wings to provide further location. The pilot's job would be to fly the plane, arm the explosives and send a signal to the mother ship to take over control. The other crew member had to tune the autopilot. They would then both bail out before the plane approached our coast.

The RAF had insisted that the drones be located in a far corner of the airfield with their personnel nearby, which caused some resentment. The lack of facilities and remoteness of the Woodbridge site meant it was not popular with the Americans. By 10 July, seven drones were loaded with nitro-starch explosive and ready to go, along with an eighth that would carry gel-gas (napalm). Poor weather conditions prevented the mission. On the same day, General Partridge of the USAAF and Duncan Sandys, now head of the Crossbow Committee for counter-measures, visited the airfield.[5]

On 12 July the pilots were briefed for a mission but again poor weather conditions saw it cancelled. An event the next day would spell the end of the US operations at RAF Woodbridge. The sound they heard in the early hours of the morning appeared to be that of unsynchronised engines, which could mean a German plane.[6] The FIDO (Fog Investigation and Dispersal Operation) was turned on, which created two rows of burning petroleum alongside the runway to burn off the fog. The plane that eventually landed was a lost German Junkers JU88, running low on fuel. Fitted with all the latest radar technology, it was of great interest to our scientists. The Americans were far more concerned that the Aphrodite presence there might have been relayed to Germany, and the whole operation compromised. The next

Following the landing of this Junkers JU88 at RAF Woodbridge on 13 July 1944, Operation Aphrodite swiftly transferred to RAF Fersfield in Norfolk.

day the decision was made to find a new location and move out of Woodbridge as quickly as possible.

The drones were all unloaded and over three days were flown to an unused RAF base near Diss, named Fersfield. The new Commanding Officer was Lt Col Roy Forrest. It was a frustrating time as missions were continually being scrubbed due to poor weather, with cloud cover meaning the drone could not be seen by the mother ship. The confinement of all personnel to base for security did not help. The operation until then had been run by the Army, but then specialist radio control units arrived from the Navy as well as the Army.

The weather finally cleared and 4 August was the day when four drones emerged from their camouflage nets and launched against the heavy sites at Watten, Siracourt, Wizernes and Mimoyecques. It was a major undertaking, which included a diversionary attack by 250 RAF bombers on targets north of Paris. Accompanying the drones were 16 P-38 Lightnings to cover the mother ships, observation and navigation B-17s with fighter cover, four P-38 photo planes, along with two Mosquitoes to photograph the pilots exiting the drones and two squadrons of Spitfires.

There were major concerns about a drone losing control. Should this occur, the mother ship had instructions to head it out to sea and have the fighters shoot it down. The risk of a drone landing on Ipswich or Norwich was the ultimate nightmare for the planners.

This operation involved the largest airborne quantity of explosives ever assembled at that time. The first take-off was to be at 13.45, with the second drone five minutes later. They would initially fly a rectangular route with checkpoints over Orfordness, Southwold and Eye before commencing the final run out. There were problems with the altimeter of the first drone which could only be controlled when it had fallen to a height of 1,200 feet. Additional problems occurred with the autopilot. By this time they were over Stowmarket, only seven minutes before their bail-out near Woodbridge. With no options open to them, the auto-pilot bailed out, and after the pilot had armed the fuses, he followed.

The drone was now controlled by the mother ship, but could only be made to go left, right or down; it could not climb. It would only fly at 300 feet, its specified height for crossing the Channel before reaching the target at Watten. No sooner had the drone left our coastline when it was heading for the cables of barrage balloons located at sea. These were supposed to have been lowered for this mission. There was also flak from our AA (Anti-Aircraft) guns, but somehow, the drone emerged the other side.

Eventually, the massive concrete roof at Watten came into view, but when lined up on the target the dump switch did not respond. They went round again but were faced with the same problem. As it could not be dumped on any target, it was decided to fly the drone close to the German flak batteries. On the second pass there was a massive explosion with great balls of fire, which effectively silenced those batteries.

The second drone had not been far behind the first as it approached the Suffolk coast, but went into a steep climb after which the auto-pilot bailed out. The pilot was desperately trying to keep the drone on an even course but it stalled. He was seen jumping out of the hatch but the drone and the pilot hit the ground around the same time. The location was Sudbourne Park where mature oak trees were felled up to 220 feet from the impact. The only significant wreckage was the cylinder blocks of the engines.

A third drone was readied, which took off from Fersfield after 15.00, but it was soon in trouble as it nearly flew into a formation of Liberators assembling for a mission. Extreme evasive action was needed, which could have had dire consequences for this heavily loaded plane. Later, as the drone approached Woodbridge airfield, the pilots prepared for their exit. Having armed the explosives and set the plane for its descent, the pilot was the last to leave. Such exits were very dangerous being at a speed much higher than for conventional parachute drops, and at a position very close to the propeller. This particular jump combined these hazards along with the

The 'Careful Virgin' after long service became an Aphrodite drone. It took off for its final mission on 4 August. The destination was Mimoyecques, but it became uncontrollable and crashed short of the target in a ball of fire.

static line being ripped out of the aircraft and the secondary chest-chute failing to open. Manual deployment of the shrouds provided some retardation, and the pilot was lucky to land in the branches of a tree.

The mother ship would now control the drone on its route to Wizernes. The drone was held by the altimeter at 300 feet and awaiting the control signal to send it down on the target. After it was given, the drone was seen to enter some cloud before passing over the target and exploding beyond it.

The fourth and final drone that day took off soon after 16.00, and when the pilot and auto-pilot had bailed out, the mother ship set its route for Mimoyecques. Although the purpose of this site was unknown then, it was the location of the V3 supergun. As the drone approached the French coast it became more and more uncontrollable as it kept climbing. A final attempt to reduce height resulted in it crashing short of the target in a ball of fire that rose high in the sky. The mother ship had an eventful journey home as it was caught up in V1 attacks on London and experienced the flak of our defences.

To sum up the first Aphrodite missions on 4 August; four drones were launched, one was blown up by enemy flak, one crashed and exploded in Suffolk, one crashed beyond the target and the fourth malfunctioned, hit the ground and blew up. Eight men had bailed out, one was killed and the others had various injuries.

The next mission was two days later, on 6 August 1944. A new development was the use of Torpex, a British explosive that was significantly more powerful than nitro starch and would allow a lower weight loading for the same effect. There would be only two drones this time, with a ten-minute interval, each controlled by primary and secondary mother ships. The target for both was Watten.

The first drone was loaded with Torpex while the second was filled with a mix of incendiary bombs and napalm. There would be 100 British bombers making diversionary raids, along with the usual number of support aircraft. The procedures for setting the autopilot and arming the fuses of the first drone all went well and both men successfully bailed out. One even landed next to an AA battery and was soon surrounded by female personnel, a perfect outcome. It would not be the same for the drone, which soon after passing Orfordness, did not respond correctly to the 'turn right' instruction. It promptly turned left, rolled over on its back and went into the sea.

The autopilot of the second drone was set up and control passed to the mother ship. When the pilot bailed out, his arm was caught in the static line, which caused severe injury and would eventually lead to amputation. It soon became clear that the control was not functioning correctly as the plane could not make a left turn, which was urgently needed. Attempts to pass control to the secondary mother ship were unsuccessful and the drone packed with incendiaries and napalm was seen heading in the direction of London. It then vanished from view and was lost in the hazy conditions. After about ten minutes of intense observation, the bright wings of the drone were seen again. Only now, it was doing 360 degree turns over Ipswich and the surrounding area. Further adjustments to the controls were made but visual contact was again lost. When re-established, the drone was circling over the eastern area of Ipswich.

A series of control manoeuvres finally allowed the drone to reach the coastline but it was then lost in fog. They had narrowly avoided a major disaster, so when the drone was seen over mudflats near the estuary, it was dumped. A massive ball of yellow flame shot into the air. The radio operator shouted out "the whole North Sea's on fire", which prompted a reply from the controller, "Better than Ipswich".

It would now be the turn of the US Navy. The Army's Double Azon control system would be replaced by their own FM-TV which they had been developing for some time. The Navy was all set to fly their first mission from Fersfield and, as might be expected, there were considerable tensions between the Army and the Navy. The Navy's first drone was not a B-17 but their version of the B-24 Liberator, designated PB4Y-1. This was a brand-new Liberator that was fully stripped out in America and then ferried to England. There were several delays before everything was ready for their first mission on 12 August 1944, which would be to Mimoyecques.

The pilot for this mission was Lt Joseph Kennedy Jnr. He was the eldest son of the former US ambassador to Britain, whose family moved in the upper circles of American society. His father had ambitions for him to become US President. Joe was a battle-hardened pilot though, having completed two tours of duty in Liberators. Although the control equipment in the PB4Y-1 was in the main superior to that of the Army, doubts had been expressed about the arming panel that looked a bit too home-made. Lt Col Forrest referred to it "being as safe as a basketful of rattlesnakes". The Navy crew in the mother ship would arm the drone after the jump crew had bailed out, so potentially it was a much safer system. Concerns still remained that stray FM signals might be able to arm the drone and that there could be problems with the arming panel.

Lt Joseph Kennedy Jnr was pilot of the Operation Anvil Liberator that blew up south of Blythburgh on 12 August 1944.

The Navy was using TV cameras in the drone to allow the controller in the Ventura mother ship to guide it to the target. This would obviate the frightening situation of loosing visual contact when clouds intervened. Kennedy had carried out many test flights in the Liberator loaded with sand as ballast to simulate the weight of explosives, with the mother ship successfully controlling it. Lt Olsen, an electronics expert, had grave concerns about the inadequacies of the arming panel, but after prolonged and heated discussions with senior personnel, including Lt Wilford Willy who would be the auto-pilot, there was no approval to make the necessary safety modifications. As a last resort, Kennedy himself was drawn into the discussions but was not in a position to intervene.

The mission originally planned for 11 August was scrubbed due to poor weather conditions. The next day the whole armada of support planes was ready. Kennedy started the engines of PB4Y-1 No. 32271 and taxied to the runway, and with Willy beside him made a perfect take-off. Technicians on the ground crowded around the TV receiver, on which they saw the unfolding check route of the drone. From Saxmundham, they made a left turn for the next check-point over Beccles, passing over Theberton and Blythburgh.

The TV pictures suddenly flickered and died, quickly followed by two massive explosions which lit up the sky. The yellow nucleus turned to a greenish white cylinder of fire shaped like an hour-glass. One of the Ventura mother ships was sent into a dive and only just pulled out before hitting the ground. A Mosquito camera plane piloted by Bob Tunnel flew through the centre and despite being damaged was lucky to survive. The observer Dan McCarthy later described what happened[7] "…the Baby just exploded in mid-air as we neared it and I was knocked halfway back to the cockpit. A few pieces of the Baby came through the plexiglass nose and I got hit in the head and caught a lot of fragments in my right arm. I crawled back to the cockpit and lowered the wheels so that Bob could make a quick emergency landing."

Kennedy and Willy were killed in the explosion 2½ miles north-west of Dunwich over Hinton Lodge. Many houses were damaged over a wide area along with churches at Blythburgh, Thorington, Walberswick and Wangford. Bulcamp Red House Institution, Henham Hall and Saint Felix School also suffered damage.[8] Several people received injuries but there was no loss of life on the ground. Remnants of the plane were scattered over Newdelight Woods and Westwood Marshes, while one engine was found at Blythburgh Lodge and the other three at Hinton Lodge.

The explosion was heard over a wide area and the period leading up to it was keenly observed by nine-year-old Mick Muttitt and his brother Peter while playing in their garden at Dresser's Cottage in Darsham. Mick took a great interest in aircraft and soon recognised a Liberator at the head of a formation of aircraft passing close to the east. He takes up the story.

Bomb-bay doors of the Liberator. Parham Airfield Museum (PAM).

I immediately attempted to identify the accompanying types and listed two Hudsons (which I now know were Venturas), two Lightnings, two Flying Fortresses and a Mosquito. Several local Mustangs flew at a discreet distance. As this unique assembly passed by at about 1,500 ft, a thin trail of smoke was discernible coming from the rear of the Liberator's weapons bay. Then I watched in horror as the lead aircraft exploded in a huge fireball. I vividly remember seeing burning wreckage falling earthwards while engines with propellers still turning, and leaving comet-like trails of smoke, continued along the direction of flight before plummeting down. A Ventura broke high to starboard and a Lightning spun away to port eventually to regain control at tree-top height over Blythburgh Hospital. While I watched spellbound a terrific explosion reached Dresser's Cottage in the form of a loud double thunderclap. Then all was quiet except for the drone of the circling Venturas' engines, as they remained for a few more minutes in the vicinity. The fireball changed to an enormous black pall of smoke resembling a huge octopus, the tentacles below indicating the earthward path of burning fragments.

Endless investigations and reports all concluded that the Navy's arming panel was faulty. As the Allies overran the four major sites that were assumed to be manufacturing the V-weapons, it quickly became clear that they had all been abandoned some time ago, but a token presence convincingly led to the conclusion that they were still operating. Bomber Command carried out further heavy attacks on 25 and 27 August.[9] The latter was an accurate raid on Mimoyecques by 176 Halifax, 40 Lancaster and 10 Mosquito bombers.[10]

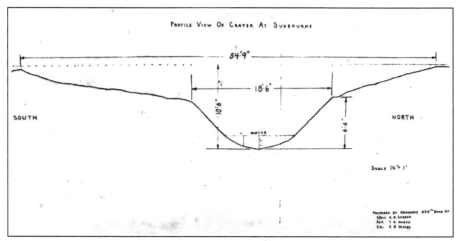

One drone crashed on 4 August at Sudbourne. The dimensions of the crater were recorded by 390th Bomb Group Ordnance personnel so that the effectiveness of the explosives could be determined. PAM.

'Gremlin Gus' was another Flying Fortress that would become a drone in the later period of the Aphrodite programme, with a cut-down fuselage and windshield fitted.

There would be a further Anvil mission, to the U-Boat pens on the island of Heligoland, but that also failed when the plane exploded on a coal pile near the entrance to the submarine pens. This spelt the end of their programme. The Army was keen to press on and were developing a drone with the upper part of the fuselage and cockpit removed to accommodate special hydrostatic bombs to attack the German battleship *Turpitz*, but Barnes Wallis's Tallboy bombs got there first. There were further unsuccessful missions to Heligoland and on 27 January 1945 the whole programme was halted.

The Aphrodite and Anvil projects were conceived as the American's way to neutralise the massive structures that the Nazis had constructed for their V-weapons. Unbeknown to the Allies, the Tallboy bombs had effectively achieved that destruction. The population of Suffolk in particular, had been put at great risk. One drone exploded in an unpopulated area, another loaded with napalm came close to incinerating part of Ipswich, while Kennedy's plane self-destructed over Newdelight Woods. The name hardly fits with this disastrous event.

Parham Airfield Museum (www.parhamairfieldmuseum.co.uk), the Norfolk and Suffolk Aviation Museum (www.aviationmuseum.net) and the Holton Airfield Memorial Museum (halesworthairfieldmuseum.co.uk), all have relics associated with this incident.

Notes

1. Grehan, J., *Hitler's V-Weapons, An Official History*, Frontline Books, 2020, pp. 135, 325.
2. Engelmann, J., *V2 Dawn of the Rocket Age*, Schiffer Publishing, 1990, p. 44.
3. The National Archives (TNA), AIR 28–294, RAF Woodbridge ORB.
4. Kinsey, G., *Bawdsey, Birth of the Beam*, Terence Dalton, 1983, p. 114.
5. Ibid., 3.
6. Olsen, Jack, *Aphrodite, Desperate Mission*, Putnam, 1970, the main source for this chapter.
7. Imperial War Museum (IWM), photo caption, FRE 595.
8. Norfolk & Suffolk Aviation Museum.
9. Ibid., 1, p. 135.
10. Middlebrook and Everitt, *The Bomber Command War Diaries*, Ian Allen Publishing, 1985, p. 111.

Attacking the V1s and Heinkels

In Phase 1 of the attacks (13 June to 1 September), the V1s were predominantly launched from land-based ramps during the day and night. The RAF's task was to shoot them down as they approached the coast or passed over land. One Suffolk pilot was directly involved in the early confrontations with the V1. Stanley Chambers grew up in Ipswich and joined the RAF as a medical orderly in 1937. His ambition was to fly, so in 1940 he volunteered for pilot training. The next year he went to Canada under The British Government Air Training Plan and on his return made his first flight in a Spitfire. Over the next two years he gained much experience on various aircraft. He flew PRU sorties over Europe at considerable risk, the aircraft being unarmed.

165 Squadron with Stanley Chambers moved to RAF Detling in Kent as part of Operation Diver. The Squadron set up 24-hour patrols as the V1s were being launched around the clock. Within their duty period they would fly up to four sorties a day. In the early days of the Diver campaign the pilots were at risk from our own AA fire against the V1s and also from our barrage balloons. Changes were soon made to the location of the guns and balloons to address this problem.

The Squadron was equipped with the Mark IX Spitfire and was credited with destroying 59 V1s. The Spitfire was not as powerful as the Hawker Tempest, the dominant aircraft at the time, but it still achieved good results. Stanley was in the thick of it and observed.

> When we got onto flying bombs we often had dusk or night landings. All you could see was the fire from the Spitfire's Merlin engine's exhaust, you can't see anything else, it's all flame! It was awful, you couldn't see a thing! And you're coming in and it's dark! So, what they had to put was proper flame shields [dampers] over the exhaust to cut out the glare! And there's no flare-path [along the runway], they wouldn't put it on. We were on the coast; a German might be following you in for all you knew.

Stanley noted that the V1 could be seen from some distance, "bloody great jet flame out the back of the flying bomb. You could see it from miles away". However, the pilots were dependent on the vector information supplied by the radar stations to get them to the right location in order to see that flame.

His first successful encounter with a V1 was on 27 June. The incident report stated, 'picked up the bomb due south of Pevensey, one mile out to sea, IAS [indicated air speed] 300 mph, height 2,500 feet, course 350 degrees. Gave several short

Stanley Chambers from Ipswich with his Spitfire Mk Vc in 1943. He went on to shoot down two V1s with the later Mk 1X Spitfire.

bursts and saw numerous strikes. Bomb crashed between Tunbridge Wells and Tonbridge, just over railway line and exploded on ground at 18.20 approximately'. The excitement of claiming his first V1 was tempered by the controller's claim that it was shared with a Hawker Tempest V, which was not well received.

In the heat of battle it was the pilot who made the decisions. Stanley observed, "As a fighter pilot you had to use your own initiative. You make up your own rules. You're your own boss. You make the decisions, nobody else." Some adopted the method of tipping the V1's wing to destabilise it, causing it to crash. Stanley was not in favour of this because of the risk to his own aircraft, which could have prevented him from further flying. An earlier 165 Squadron Leader attempted to flip a V1 but misjudged the angle, striking and detonating the bomb. His Spitfire was destroyed and he was killed.

Relocation of 165 Squadron to RAF Lympne near Hythe in Kent placed them in 'Doodlebug Alley'. Several V1s fell on the base, causing loss of life and damage to buildings. Stanley saw much action against the V1s and claimed his second one on 28 July, which exploded on the ground.

I remember seeing it coming in and being directed by the controller. Gunsight is on fire, you press the button, go round, and you shoot him. I went round and had a look at the blast. It went through a house and the

V1 landed at the bottom of the garden. And I remember the two walking out to have a look at it. They were OK — I remember having a look because I waggled my wings.

In August the squadron moved back to Detling and started escort duties, which saw the end of Stanley's V1-chasing days. The main airfields in the eastern counties associated with V1 interceptions were RAF Coltishall in Norfolk, RAF Castle Camps in Cambridge, close to the Suffolk border, and RAF Bradwell Bay in Essex.

Throughout 1944, 45 different squadrons of the Coltishall Wing were involved with missions against the V1 and V2.[1] Mosquitoes were dispatched in pairs at two-hourly intervals and were successful in destroying V1s in southern England. In June, the peak (2,453 incidents) of V1 activity against England, many were destroyed by fighter planes, including 50 in that month by 316 (Polish) Squadron.[2]

Most of the ramp-launched V1s in Phase 1 crossed the south coast. From September 1944 these launch-sites had all been overrun by the Allies and the Germans were now reliant on launching them from Heinkel aircraft in the hours of darkness. Once the V1 had been launched, the options to destroy it were twofold: shoot it down by AA fire, or attack it by aircraft. Phase 2 brought Norfolk and Suffolk into the firing line as the V1s now passed overhead on their way to London.

Score board for 25 Squadron RAF Coltishall, showing eight He 111 destroyed from 25 September along with two probables. Neatishead Radar Museum.

The slow-moving Heinkel 111 with its V1 fixed below the wing would have been an easy target in daylight, so their sorties were carried out in the hours of darkness. The twin-engine de Havilland Mosquito was the ideal night-fighter for intercepting it, along with the Hawker Tempest Mk V based at Bradwell Bay.[3] The preference was to intercept the Heinkel before it could launch its weapon, but that aim was fraught with difficulty. The carrier planes flew very low, dropping to around 300 feet above the sea and could be detected only when they rose up for the launch, which left only a short time for the fighter to be vectored onto it.

Also the slow speed of the Heinkel was below the stall speed of the Mosquito, which often led to overshooting. On 5 November a 68 Squadron Mosquito was in contact with a He 111 but overshot it at 160 mph. On the second contact the wheels and flaps were lowered to reduce speed but still remain above stall. Soon after the Heinkel released the V1 but the glare from its exhaust caused the pilot to temporarily loose his night vision. The Mosquito pilot was still able to follow the bomber as it tried to evade the radar but was soon caught and despatched with a two-second burst from its guns. Bristol Blenheim aircraft were also used for Heinkel chasing as their stall speed was lower than the Mosquito. There was a period of around ten seconds when the V1 pulse jet was started, prior to launch, when the Heinkel was illuminated and particularly vulnerable to attack.[4]

The NF.XXX de Havilland Mosquitoes of 25 Squadron were successful in shooting down He 111s at night.

Model of He 111 with V1 suspended below wing. N&S Aviation Museum.

There were many occasions when aircraft from Coltishall successfully attacked the intruding enemy planes with their deadly cargo. Wg Cdr Mitchell and Fl Lt Cox in their Mosquito NF.XV11 claimed 25 Squadron's first He 111 on 25 September although it was recorded as a 'probable'. Four days later there would be no doubt. They took off at 00.55 on 29 September.

> At 3,500 feet, 40 miles east of Great Yarmouth the crew witnessed a V1 being launched from the He 111 mother ship. As Wg Cdr Mitchell dived on the enemy, Greyfriars Control informed him that the He 111 was also making a port turn. The Mosquito levelled off at 600 feet in a turn and Fl Lt Cox made contact with the enemy on his ALX. The 'blip' on the radar identified the raider as being at two and a half miles range. The Mosquito descended further to 200 feet above the waves, and at 1,300 feet away from the Heinkel they gained visual contact. With his night-vision glasses, Fl Lt Cox confirmed the contact as a He 111-22. From 400 feet astern, Wg Cdr Mitchell let fly with a short burst from the Mosquitoe's guns, scoring a direct hit. The Heinkel exploded, disgorging debris and wreckage into the path of the Mosquito. Mitchell turned hard right to avoid the mortally wounded He 111. Turning full circle the Mosquito crew saw the doomed bomber crash in flames into the North Sea where it burned for a few minutes before sinking.

Painting by Frank Leyland of V1 shortly after launch from He 111.

Soon after, they saw another V1 being launched. They were rapidly gaining on the mother ship, their speed being 220 mph compared with about 180– 190 mph for the Heinkel. After two separate bursts from their guns, the plane suffered the same fate as the previous one.[5]

In Phase 2, 26 He 111s were destroyed by fighter aircraft. Although the V1s were normally launched a long way from our coast, there were instances when the launch was very close. On 23 December at 06.51, 'An aircraft plotted as friendly and showing navigation lights approached to within 2,000 yds of the coast just south of Lowestoft where it released a flying bomb which was too close for engagement.'[6]

Weather conditions had a significant effect on the ability to send up aircraft. On 30 October, a Coltishall detachment was on standby at Bradwell Bay. The crews were asked if they were prepared to fly as the fog was dense. They took off, hardly able to see the runway lights and were soon engulfed in the fog. Despite these difficult conditions, they destroyed two Heinkels but ran out of ammunition just as another launched its V1. They were fortunate to land back at Coltishall when a brief 'hole' appeared in the fog.[7]

There were many USAAF Fighter Groups located in Norfolk and Suffolk who escorted bombers on their raids to the V-weapon sites, but 'flying bomb catching was chiefly in the realm of RAF fighters.'[8]

The destruction of the V1s was down to the combined attacks of the RAF and AA Command. Appendix VII shows the relative numbers of V1s which were shot down in Phase 2 of the campaign, between September 1944 and January 1945.

The presence of such great numbers of AA guns along the coast combined with the advantages of the proximity fuse and gun-laying radar, inevitably led to them making the greater number of kills.

Notes

1. Jennings, M., *RAF Coltishall*, Old Forge Publishing, 2007, p. 284.
2. Ibid., p.119.
3. Smith, P., *Air-Launched Doodlebugs*, Pen and Sword Aviation, 2006, pp. 47, 48.
4. Ibid., pp. 24, 25.
    Ibid., 1, pp. 123, 128, 129.
5. Ibid., 1, p.125.
6. The National Archives (TNA), WO 166/14671, 63 Brigade, Royal Artillery.
7. Ibid., 1, p. 69.
    TNA, AIR 27/93, 125 Squadron ORB.
8. Freeman, R., *The Mighty Eighth, a History of the U. S. Army Air Force*, Macdonald and Jane's, 1978, p. 169.

Operation Diver

The military name assigned to the V1 was Diver, hence the Diver Operation that started in June 1944 and finished in March 1945. The defences around our coasts to combat the V1s were complex and fast moving. AA guns had been in action against enemy aircraft throughout the war, but from June 1944 they were taking on a new form of aircraft that did not have a pilot to guide it. The V1 flew in a straight line at a fairly constant speed, which should have made it an ideal target for the AA guns. However, there were many problems to address, but in the final phase when the guns had moved to the east coast (the Diver Strip) an effective system had been developed to shoot down a high proportion of the V1s trying to cross our coastline.

The active period of the whole Diver campaign encompassed only 290 days, but the movement of the AA sites and the introduction of new equipment was a remarkable achievement. To gain some insight into this campaign we need to go back to June 1944 when the first V1s were launched from ramps in the Pas de Calais area of France. AA guns were already located around major towns, ports and vital areas to defend against conventional bombing raids, but their extent was massively increased to combat the new form of attack.

The ATS (Auxiliary Territorial Service) would form an important part of these defences, with women performing essential roles on the gun sites although not actually firing the guns. Joan Allen from Bury St Edmunds was in the ATS and worked on the searchlights near the Straits of Dover. She got to learn much about the activities in 'Fly Bomb Alley'. When the attacks began, all leave was cancelled, and until they ceased it was duty every night, with sleep snatched during the day.[1] The local Home Guard also played an increasing role with the AA guns as younger men were being transferred for front-line duty abroad.

The approach to defending London comprised a barrage-balloon belt to the south and the Kentish Gun Belt, with fighter planes in the zone to the coast. The Balloon Command was formed in 1938 and by the end of the war there were several thousand balloons in use protecting towns, cities, industrial areas and ports from attack by enemy aircraft. The balloons were inflated with hydrogen and were approximately 66 feet long and 25 feet in diameter. They were attached by steel cable to a winch and flew at a height of around 6,000 feet. They were in place during the Blitz but later had a role in combating the V1.

In Norfolk and Suffolk there were a number of barrage balloon sites in place to combat hostile aircraft. Norwich suffered badly from conventional bombing, particularly during the Baedeker raids in April 1942. The number of balloons in

Barrage balloons accounted for nearly 6 per cent of all V1s knocked down, and were part of the defences of London. These balloons guarding Felixstowe harbour are from earlier in the war and not part of Diver defences.

the area was increased, with sites numbered up to 36. There were approximately 19 sites in Ipswich. RAF Felixstowe was a base for barrage balloons and served mainly by WAAFs. There were 24 balloons, 12 of which were anchored to barges in Harwich Haven. In the early years of the war, balloons were flown from trawlers of the RN patrol service in Lowestoft. After 1943 a further dozen land-based balloons were used, tethered to sites along the seafront. Balloons had to be raised and lowered depending on the weather and when conditions were bad they had to be grounded.[2]

Nationally, barrage balloons accounted for about 231 downed V1s.[3] Although it was a matter of luck whether a V1 would strike a balloon, they had been in use since the early part of the war, providing a boost to the morale in

Bofors 40mm LAA gun on south coast, August 1944. It was the shell from a Bofors gun that hit the House in the Clouds in Thorpeness on 5 November. © IWM, H39805.

the areas where they were sited. The balloons formed an important belt around southern London to combat the V1s but were not specifically used to protect areas in the Diver Strip.

Later versions of the V1 were fitted with a sawtooth arrangement on the wing, designed to cut the balloons' retaining cables which were also a risk to Allied aircraft. In 1942, the Belgian pilot of a Spitfire hit a balloon cable while flying over Norwich and died in the ensuing crash.[4] A total of around 100 aircraft were brought down by balloons, of which 75 per cent were Allied planes. This is a shocking figure but it has to be set against the far greater number of Allied planes operating over Britain compared with German planes.[5]

The first V1s made their appearance on 13 June flying in a north-westerly direction. The signal to deploy guns to the Kentish Gun Belt was given on 16 June. The next day 113 V1s arrived over the coast, with 29 being destroyed by gunfire. The average speed of the V1 was around 345 mph although individual speeds exceeding 400 mph were observed. The average height was 2,500 feet, within a range of 1,000 to 4,000 feet.

It soon became evident that this was a difficult height for the guns. Light Anti-Aircraft (LAA) were not able to elevate their guns to that height, while Heavy Anti-

ATS girls with height and range finder at Weybourne. Muckleburgh Military Collection (MMC).

Aircraft (HAA) could not lower their guns sufficiently. There were also complex issues with radar interception of the bombs, with different types of equipment being available, and the effects of the surroundings influencing the outcome. The use of spotters with binoculars was still an important part of early detection. In addition to the guns there were six squadrons of Spitfires and two of Tempests for V1 patrols.

LAA regiments were deployed on the south coast with Bofors 40mm guns and also lighter Hispano Suiza 20mm guns. This arrangement caused some difficulties as Category B strikes (V1 hit by AA fire and keeps going for some time) could impact in residential areas. Along with restrictions on some AA Commands, the situation needed to be reviewed, with the outcome being that the HAA guns would move to the coast from 15/16 July. This would be known as the Coastal Gun Belt, stretching from near Newhaven (Cuckmere Haven) to Dover (St Margaret's Bay), covering a distance of some 60 miles.

An important development related to trials of a proximity fuse, called Bonzo, which became available from mid July. This was a British invention that was developed by the Americans. It consisted of an assembly of miniature radar components located in the nose of the shell, which was activated on discharge from the gun. This would become a defining element of future Diver strategy as the ability for a shell to explode near its target rather than after a timed fuse setting meant greater numbers of V1s could be destroyed.

Heavy artillery was provided by the Vickers 3.7-inch gun, initially as a mobile unit and then as a static one, being more stable and with a greater flexibility in its bearings of fire. The static gun did require a substantial base, but with rapid relocation, concrete bases were not a practical option. The answer lay in the 'Pile portable platform',[6] named after General Sir Frederick Pile who had been appointed founding head of AA Command in 1939. It essentially consisted of railway sleepers with tie rods and track fixed at right angles to form a rigid base, backfilled with 50 tons of ballast. These foundations were successfully used throughout the campaign.

The decision to move to the coast had major implications but was clearly the right one, for guns could now fire out to sea without risk to inland areas and friendly aircraft. The logistics were quite overwhelming: some 23,000 men and women needed to relocate and be ready for action on 19 July. Even before the move, V1 plots had been noted as coming from an easterly direction. Their significance was not known at the time but plans were being made to counter them. It soon became apparent the plots originated from aircraft- launched V1s and not ramp launched.

To counteract the new direction of attack the Coastal Belt was extended beyond Deal. The number of V1 attacks had decreased and there were periods with no traffic at all. Duncan Sandys, now chairman of the Crossbow Committee for V-Weapon counter-measures announced in the press on 7 September that, "except possibly for a few last parting shots, what has come to be known as the battle for London is over." The *East Anglian Daily Times* was quick to report on 8 September that 'Britain may be Bomb Free in 14 Days'.

The predictor was used by the ATS to calculate how far the guns would need to fire in front of the V1 in order to hit it. MMC.

There had been a sense that the V1 campaign was over and there would be no more such incidents until 15 September. However, on the evening of 8 September the first V2 struck, exploding in Chiswick and killing three people. The V2 attacks would continue until late March 1945, with a total of 1,115.[7] There would also be over 600 more air-launched V1s that would approach our coast up to 14 January, along with renewed ramp launches in March.

Searchlights were fixed on tracks in order that they could be readily moved. They were used to track aircraft and V1s. MMC.

The defences around the Thames and Medway were strengthened and formed what became known as the Diver Box, extending from Herne Bay through Chatham to Chelmsford and Clacton. The plots of the incoming V1s showed they made landfall over Essex, which created difficulties in that any extension of the defences would potentially conflict with the large numbers of Allied bombers that operated in the same airspace.

On 20 September, the Heinkels of 111/KG 3 despatched V1s that crossed the coast south of Lowestoft, which was a new departure. In Felixstowe, Inspector Rush noted 'about 7 V-1s passing over or close to Felixstowe going SW.' Orders were issued the same day that the existing guns at Yarmouth and Lowestoft were to be reinforced. V1s continued to be launched in the hours of darkness, but failures kept down the number to actually reach the coast. There was uncertainty concerning the extent of future attacks.

The outcome of an ADGB (Air Defence of Great Britain) meeting on 21 September was to extend the defences further northwards, based on a likely limit of V1s crossing the coast at Yarmouth. The new area was called the Eastern Diver Gun Strip, or just Diver Strip, and extended from Clacton to Newport, north of Yarmouth, a distance of some 65 miles. The southern battle of the V1s was over and the east coast now became the focus of attention.

Notes

1. *Bury Free Press*, 10 November 1944.
2. Osborne, M., and Graham Keer, A., *20th Century Defences in Britain, Suffolk*, Concrete Publications, 2008, p. 119.
   Grehan, J., *Hitler's V-Weapons, An Official History*, Frontline Books, 2020, p. 119.
3. Collier, B., *The Defence of The United Kingdom*, HMSO and Longmans Green, 1957, Appendix XLV.
4. www.aircrewremembered.com.
5. *Britain at War*, Key Publishing, December 2022, p. 83.
6. Dobinson, C., *Operation Diver*, Historic England, 2019, p.183.
7. Ibid., 2, Grehan, J., Appendix XVIII.

The Diver Strip

This chapter covers the development of the Diver Strip in Norfolk and Suffolk. The southern extremity of the Strip was at Thorpe-le-Soken in Essex. The history of the Diver campaign, like everything in wartime, was one of constant change. It was no different in the Diver Strip and the format of the defences and the personnel changed throughout this phase of the campaign. Many personnel were required for the gun sites since it was not only the guns but also searchlights, predictors, height finders, radar sets and communication equipment that had to be operated. By August 1944, Home Guard personnel made up nearly half of the gun crews.

Official reports provide factual information on the activity in the Diver Strip, but for a personal account throughout the period, the diaries of Tom King provide an important resource. In May 1940 he became an ARP warden in Southwold. He was disabled following a teenage accident when kicked by a horse, which ultimately led to his leg being amputated. From July 1940, his role changed to that of ARP telephonist at the police station. He was therefore, in a unique position to gather information on all activities in Southwold and the surrounding area. His diaries, *My Second World War Dairies in Southwold by Tom King*, were anonymously published some time after his death, and extracts have been used in this book.

There were two types of AA defence: heavy artillery (HAA) and light artillery (LAA). Both were in use at the start of the Diver Strip along with hybrid sites that used various combinations of both, but it soon became apparent that the HAA with its superior range was able to engage V1s before they came within range of the lighter 40mm Bofors guns. By the last week of November there were only eight LAA guns remaining in the Strip, the others having been withdrawn. There were 346 HAA guns including those in Essex, mainly located on four-gun sites. The separation between each gun on an HAA site was 30 yards, while the typical distance between batteries was 1,100 yards where the terrain allowed. They were to be as near to the coast as possible.

The predominant form of HAA battery in the Diver Strip consisted of four 3.7-inch power-turned Vickers Mk 2 C static guns on Pile foundations, firing VT98 (Bonzo) proximity-fused shells. The latest auto-tracking gun-laying radar was the American SCR 584, which in combination with the No 10 predictor increased the kill ratio from 1/2,500 rounds to 1/100 rounds fired. The V1s were coming over at even lower heights, sometimes below 1,000 feet, which necessitated the flank guns being modified so that they could fire down to an elevation of just 5 degrees and were initially located in front of the central guns to form an arc. This was later changed to a straight-line layout.

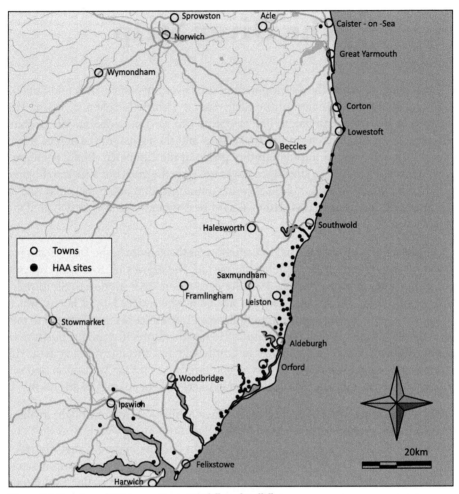

Figure 6.1. Location of HAA gun sites in Norfolk and Suffolk.

Searchlights were an important part of V1 detection. Female searchlight batteries were not allowed to bear arms, and pickaxe handles would have been used to defend the perimeter. There was, though, a married man who lived in a tent on the site whose job was to start the generator, but even he disappeared after electric starting was introduced. In the Diver Strip the spacing between searchlights was approximately 3,000 yards. They generally operated in a restricted arc to prevent dazzling gun sites. A 'one beam' rule required the first searchlight to be doused when a second beam took over.[1]

Tom King noted, '10 November, …Fly went in just north of the town, the searchlight at Easton switched inland and made a fine sight as it touched the top of buildings and trees for miles inland, the Fly was exploded well inland.' In practice, coastal towns and villages, along with river estuaries, would all influence the layout that could be achieved for the guns and searchlights.

At the outset of the Diver Strip it was not intended that there would be mixed units with women of the ATS, due to the potential difficulties of providing accommodation in the forthcoming winter. However, mixed units were arriving by early October and were duly accommodated. There were concerns from mothers about their daughters mixing with so many single young men. This resulted in middle-aged married men being used but they found the girls to be silly and the men were found to be boring, so that idea was abandoned.

Moving equipment and personnel from the south to the Strip would turn out to be a logistical nightmare. Previous moves had taken place over four to five days, but now they were faced with crossing the Thames, moving along a limited number of main roads and then heading off into the lanes of Suffolk. Transport was a serious problem with few heavy vehicles available to tow the guns and equipment. Those vehicles then had to return to pick up more equipment, and the outcome of these vehicles meeting each other on narrow winding lanes in the dark can well be imagined.

The guns needed to be located as close to the coast as possible, but the preferred positions were often near marshland which could only be accessed by tracks that quickly became a sea of mud. Pile summed up the situation, "The deployment to Diver Strip has been deplorable… and reflects great discredit on every one of us…"[2] Conditions in the remote sites were basic and arduous. Fresh water in many cases had to be brought in by carts and it took some days before electric light and telephones were connected. Bad weather saw tents and marquees blown down. The new gun locations would need Pile foundations, which were manufactured by REME (Royal Electrical and Mechanical Engineers) at the 14th AA workshops in Hadleigh, Suffolk.[3]

The following observations are made on some HAA gun positions located along the coast:

G1-14 were located along the coast between Bawdsey and Orford. G4 was close to Orford Quay while the remainder were in isolated positions that would have been very difficult to reach with no metalled roads, only tracks. The War Diary of 189 HAA recorded on 23 October '…visited G1 and G2…mud everywhere and want at least 100 tons of hardcore per site…Went on to G3. Sea of mud and could not get on to G4.'[4]

S4 was near the railway line passing Thorpeness and potentially firing over Thorpeness.

T7 and 14 were close to Leiston on the coast side, and the noise of these guns would have been very loud at the nearest houses not far away.

T13 and 20 were very close to Walberswick, while T12 was on Southwold Common. A Category A explosion over the town on 14 October caused extensive damage to

HAA 3.7-inch guns on Gedgrave marshes with Orford Castle in background. These are likely posed or practice photos as the V1s only appeared in the hours of darkness. © IWM, H40431.

Crews head for the guns on Southwold Common. The view is towards the river with the towers of Darsham CH radar station just visible above the gun on the right. © IWM, 40434.

many properties in Southwold.

YH1 and 2 were the most northerly in the Strip and were part of the original GDA (Gun Defended Area) of the Yarmouth defences. YH1 was in Gorleston while YH2 was about 1 ½ miles inland at Caister-on-Sea.

Many locations though, were in fairly remote areas where shell fragments would fall into the sea and few people lived nearby. The gun belt covered a distance of 10,000 yards out to sea and 5,000 yards inland. The Diver Strip was divided into five sections as follows:

The HAA guns were mounted on Pile platforms, seen here under construction at the REME workshops in Hadleigh.
© IWM, H39586.

40 AA Brigade from Thorpe (near Clacton) to Bawdsey, under Brigadier Krohn with HQ at West Bergholt.

102 AA Brigade from Bawdsey to Orford, under Brigadier Harrison with HQ at The Gables, Orford.

5 AA Brigade from Orford to Leiston, under Brigadier Rowbotham with HQ at Hurts Hall, Saxmundham.

57 AA Brigade from Leiston to Benacre, under Brigadier Chichester-Cooke with HQ at Theberton Hall.

63 AA Brigade from Benacre to Newport, north of Yarmouth, under Brigadier Paris, with HQ at Marine Parade, Gorleston.

The move to the Strip, which started on 22 September, was finally complete by 13 October. Appendix VI lists 73 Diver HAA sites in Norfolk and Suffolk on one particular day, 24 November 1944. The distribution of these sites is shown on Figure 6.1. The peak months for V1s approaching the coast were October (203) and November (188), therefore that date is representative of a time when there was significant action. Information on other times and also LAA sites can be found in *Operation Diver*.[5]

There were already guns located around major towns and ports known as Gun Defended Areas (GDA). The Harwich GDA extended to cover Nacton and Martlesham airfields, Landguard, Trimley St Martin and Bawdsey radar station.[6]

The approach of winter in 1944 meant that accommodation would be needed for large numbers of personnel. The conditions on most sites were challenging. © IWM, H40795.

Further up the coast there was the Lowestoft/Yarmouth GDA. Diver guns were located on these sites, but there is some uncertainty whether they were on the Ipswich sites H12, 14, 16, 18.[7]

Great knowledge had been obtained through the short history of the Diver campaign and, along with the latest equipment, the destruction rate of V1s increased. The guns of 57 Brigade engaged their first V1s on 27 September. In that month 158 V1s were launched with nearly half of them never reaching the coast. The AA guns accounted for a further 18 while five were shot down by fighters. Thirteen were reported as reaching London.

On 14 October a 'Winterisation' plan for the Diver Strip was approved, for which the implementation would take ten weeks. Some 3,500 huts, 20,000 panes of glass, 373,000 concrete slabs, 500,000 concrete blocks and 60 miles of roadway were part of the materials list for the east coast.[8] The destruction of buildings in London by the V1s generated large amounts of rubble. Returning some of it to stabilise the gun sites was some form of payback.

The accommodation was built by tradesmen from AA Command Construction

ATS girls gather near the stove to knit, clean shoes, sort the blankets, read the paper and have a cigarette. Not exactly home from home, but making the best of it. © IWM, H40806.

Batteries and unskilled men from LAA Searchlight Regiments. By the end of November the framework of the huts was progressing well and by the end of the year the works were mainly finished. Life on a remote gun site in this time would have been uncomfortable. Weather conditions were often poor with torrential rain for long periods. Finding your way about in these conditions and in darkness was very challenging.

The air-launched V1s were only active at night or in the early morning, due to the strong likelihood of the Heinkel-carrier planes being shot down by fighters in daylight hours. For that reason the Diver Strip was only operational from 30 minutes after sunset until 30 minutes before sunrise. During this time, all sites had to be ready to engage the target within ten seconds of receiving the warning. There was always significant risk to life if a V1 exploded overhead or nearby, and all sites had trenches to protect troops from shrapnel.

October saw the launching of 238 V1s. Of the 203 that approached the coast, the guns shot down 103 and the fighter planes 39. Many of the V1s that were launched malfunctioned and never reached the coast. The highest monthly number of launches in Phase 2 was 316, achieved in November, but only 188 reached the coast, a 40 per cent failure rate. On 6 November, 27 launched but 9 of them failed, 17 were shot down and just one found its way to Kent.

The *East Anglian Daily Times* commented on the last night of October,[9] '

> Thousands of families in East Anglia left their breakfast tables to take shelter as the massed AA guns on the coast sent up a wall of bursting shells. Watchers saw several bombs blow up in mid-air after having been hit.'

Most early morning incidents occurred between midnight and around 05.00, long before most people were having breakfast. However, at 07.55 on 31 October, a V1 exploded on the marshes at Sudbourne. There were later incidents that morning with the last one at 08.59 in Wandsworth, London.

The latter part of November saw the number of attacks reduce considerably, with the final operation of the month being on 25 November when just four V1s were successfully launched, with three of them being shot down by AA fire. When there was a full moon, the Luftwaffe avoided sending their planes.

Operations recommenced on 5 December but their extent would never match earlier attacks or the potential numbers that were to be expected. There was no shortage of V1s as they were being fired in considerable numbers at continental targets. The likely reason is more fundamental, a shortage of fuel for the Heinkels. At the end of the month three V1s had reached London out of the 143 that had been despatched.

Tom King made many observations on events in Southwold. A selection follows:

> 25 September, 'There is some heavy AA come into the town today, they, the Soldiers I mean are on the common in tents. I believe the guns are 4.5 [3.7], if they have a go at the Fly Bombs we shall have a noisy time'.

> 5 October, 'Spent most of the morning dealing with the AA units stationed around here. They want to know about Ambulances, Doctors, Hospitals etc'.

> 20 October, 'saw one Fly Bomb come in flying fairly high…the guns opened up but the aiming was bad, some tracer shells flashed past our window and it seemed you could put your hand out and catch them'.

> 4 November, 'Had a lively evening…I had the glasses with me and picked up on one coming. The guns opened up and there was a hell of a din, the heavy AA missed but streams of light AA went up…I could see the shells

hitting it before it blew up...'.

19 November, 'Saw one launched from a plane and destroyed south of the town by guns'.

22 November, '...at 01.15 gun-fire woke me up, and then the explosion of a Fly Bomb...'

3 January, 'All clear went at 19.17, but a Fly Bomb came over town just after, and there was a hell of a din for a time, guns firing and siren on and the Fly, the guns did not hit it and it got through...'.

There were concerns that the V1 offensive would be extended to target locations further north. Reconnaissance was carried out for suitable sites including nine between Caister and Cromer, but they were never developed.[10] An exception to the normal V1 activity occurred on 24 December when 45 were launched against Manchester. Only 31 of them crossed the Lincolnshire coast to impact over a very wide area, with only one falling in the Manchester Civil Defence Area.[11]

In Phase 2, there were 608 successful V1 launches, but the combined actions of the AA guns and fighter planes knocked out 403. Of that number, 83 per cent were claimed by AA guns and 17 per cent by fighter planes. Appendix VII shows the Phase 2 data for V1s shot down by AA fire and fighter planes.

The AA guns in the Diver Strip developed into a very effective system for destroying V1s. There were three possible outcomes. A Category A strike, by AA guns or aircraft, denoted that the V1 exploded in the air, hopefully over the sea but not always. In a Category B strike the V1 was damaged and plunged to earth at some point where it exploded. This could be near the guns or many miles further inland. The third outcome saw the V1 continue on its path towards London or some deviation from it.

Appendix VIII shows data for 138 HAA Regiment in November and December 1944 for the sites at Aldeburgh, Thorpeness and Sudbourne. Their locations are shown on Figure 6.2. Between 4 November and 23 December, 82 per cent of the 104 V1s that were engaged were destroyed (Category A) or damaged (Category B). From the combined categories, 47 per cent were Category B and being damaged were most likely to deviate from their intended route and explode in locations not too far away. The average number of rounds to achieve each strike was 37. Category B strikes also represented 47 per cent of overall figures for all sites during Phase 2. The success rate was only 33 per cent in mid September, but rose to 82 per cent by late November.[12]

Life on these remote sites was challenging: arduous winter conditions along with the need to engage the target within ten seconds, all in the hours of darkness.[13] On some days there was no action but on others it was very busy. The Sudbourne sites engaged seven V1s on 18 December, destroying or damaging six of them but on the next four days there was no action.

There was always the risk that if a V1 was hit, it could land on the site (as at Aldeburgh on 5 November), along with lethal shrapnel raining down from exploding shells. Although the guns fired at night when the targets presented themselves, they did practice in the daytime. Southwold ROC was told on 27 September, 'AA firing today take precautions against splinters'.

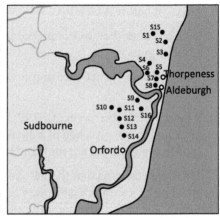

Figure 6.2. Location of HAA gun sites with reference to Appendix VIII.

There was an ever-present concern regarding the potential for friendly-fire incidents. Large formations of Allied bombers returned to their East Anglian bases through this corridor and enemy planes were known to infiltrate them. The 8th USAAF was concerned that their planes returning to Framlingham (Parham), Leiston and Martlesham were particularly at risk. Direct telephone contact was to be established between their Flying Control Towers and the local Gun Operations Room so that restrictions on fire could be quickly established.[14]

The combination of enemy planes, V1s and Allied planes in the same area was clearly a high-risk situation. On 14 November a Mosquito of 68 Squadron at RAF Coltishall was being piloted by two Americans who were gaining night-fighting experience. They were warned of an approaching enemy aircraft and turned on a course to intercept it. When the Heinkel released its V1, the Mosquito instead of following the plane as instructed, followed the V1 towards the coast and was soon caught in the searchlight beams. The AA guns opened up and the Mosquito was mortally wounded, crashing into a field at Somerleyton, killing the crew. Another Mosquito was lost to AA fire on the same night, but fortunately the crew was able to bail out safely.[15]

It is difficult to imagine what life was like for those living on the coast, certainly very different to what we are familiar with today. The coastal exclusion zone was reduced to ten miles in 1941, preventing entry unless on official business. Also, those who did not have some active role in their locality were all urged to move further inland, with the result that coastal towns might see their population fall to about a third of normal numbers.[16]

Danny Staff grew up in Thorpeness and although only nine years old at the time clearly recalled when 437 HAA Battery was located there, with its HQ at the cottage named Alnmouth. A narrow track which led to the Common was widened and compacted with gravel and rubble to provide a route for the guns to reach their positions. A number of bell tents were put up but were there only for a short time during construction of the site. Danny was able to point out the original location of the ATS huts in Thorpeness, and recalled being told off after they had thrown pebbles onto the roof of one.[17]

Danny's father Mick worked for Thorpeness Ltd and looked after the water supply, so knew all about the time when the shell from a Bofors gun struck the House in the Clouds. This iconic building is over 70 feet high and was constructed in 1923 to conceal a 30,000-gallon water tank at the top. Although there was a Bofors gun close to the tower, it was a site further away on the Warren, between Thorpeness and Aldeburgh that was understood to be the culprit.

The shell hit the steelwork below the base of the water tank and was deflected upwards into it. The contents of the tank cascaded into

The House in the Clouds at Thorpeness was hit by a Bofors shell on 5 November 1944. The contents of the water tank cascaded down onto three elderly ladies living below.

the residential accommodation below where three elderly ladies lived. Mick had to climb the tower to turn off the valves to stop the inflow of water. Danny recalled the Bofors installation on the Common near his home, but felt it was only there a short time, which agrees with the evidence showing nearly all these LAA guns had departed by the end of November. On 6 November, Tom King noted in his diary, 'Heard this morning that the Fly I said hit the Water tower at Thorpeness fell in a gun pit and never exploded, it was a shell that hit the Water tower'. Thanks to Tom we know the House in the Clouds incident was on 5 November.

Although Thorpeness is known as a holiday village with houses located around the Meare, the original village is tucked away and is where the established working families lived. Some made a living through fishing but could now reach the sea only via a dedicated fisherman's gap to avoid the mined beach. Dogs would occasionally run onto the beach but that was usually a one-way journey.

Several people from Thorpeness were employed at the Garrett works in Leiston. The factory was essential to the war effort and turned out vast numbers of guns, mountings and shells. Not only did they make the shells, they also made the machinery from which they were made. In 1940, the 12-pounder naval guns they manufactured were manned to defend the town and works when invasion was considered imminent. The factory records show that in the early years of the war there were many air raid warnings, with ten bombs actually falling on the factory, but fortunately none exploded. The raid warnings reduced in 1942 and 1943, but from June 1944 they increased significantly, reaching a maximum of 41 in October.[18] Air-launched V1s approached the coast in this area, with the local AA guns destroying many of them.

The movement of the guns into the Diver Strip inevitably had an effect on the inhabitants living close by. In Thorpeness, the nearest battery of four 3.7-inch guns was only a short distance from where Danny lived and when they opened fire in the evening there was little doubt that V1s were on their way. There was no air raid siren in Thorpeness. Danny, along with his mother and youngest sister, crawled into their Morrison table shelter when the firing started and stayed there until it ceased. His father would often stand outside with his tin helmet on, to see the action, but it was a risky business.

Danny recalled that there was a hell of a bang when the guns fired, but nothing like the noise when a V1 was hit and exploded in the air.

Searchlights were located along the coast to illuminate V1s as they approached. IWM Duxford.

The author with a 3.7-inch shell case that was fired from a Thorpeness HAA gun, the location of this photo.

Each battery at this time generally had four guns[19] and each was capable of firing up to 18 hand-loaded rounds a minute,[20] which could generate an intense, almost continuous barrage when a target was fast approaching.

Two women who lived nearby in Peace Place were very concerned about shrapnel penetrating their lightweight roof. Every night, just before 7 pm, they would come to Danny's house to seek refuge. One night, one of the women needed to go to the outside toilet but the door from the house was stuck fast. When Mick was finally able to get outside he saw that a large piece of shrapnel had hit their wall and gouged out a lump of brickwork that had then jammed itself under the door. The children would go around in the daytime collecting pieces of shrapnel and any souvenirs that could be found.

The Diver Strip experienced its greatest level of activity in the period between September and January. A great number of V1s had been launched, many fell in the sea but 608 did cross the coast and 336 of them were shot down with the expenditure of around 50,000 rounds.

The last air-launched V1s against this country were on 14 January. The tally for that month was 51 successful launches, of which 30 were shot down by AA fire, 1 by fighter, 9 went astray and 11 reached London. Although this element of the campaign had fizzled out, the V1s were still having a devastating effect on the continent. Antwerp, an important port for the Allies, was hit by 5,960 V1s and V2s before March.

The concern was that ramp launching would be re-introduced from sites in Holland and Germany. This would need the V1 to have an extended range, and evidence of this was found in February when a crashed V1 was recovered in Belgium. Modifications included a lighter warhead, the use of plywood instead of metal in the wings and airframe plus additional fuel capacity, which could extend the range to 200 miles.

It was predicted that these modified ramp-launched V1s would cross the coast between the Isle of Sheppey and Orfordness, an area already covered by the Diver Box and Strip. It was felt necessary to provide still further strength by relocating batteries from the northern part of the Strip, along with two Mosquito squadrons for sea patrols and a squadron of Tempests over land during the night period. In daytime six Mustang squadrons would be split between land and sea, with the new jet-powered Meteor also patrolling over land.[21]

This final phase of the V1 campaign started on 3 March but it would be a far less ambitious effort compared with the previous ones and lasted only 27 days. The ever-present concern about the AA guns hitting the returning friendly bombers was a real one, and was heightened by the presence of enemy night fighters intercepting them. The fog of war led to a B-17 Flying Fortress, a B-24 Liberator

HAA 3.7-inch gun at Weybourne in 2013. MMC.

Night firing of guns at Weybourne in 1945. MMC.

and a Halifax being shot down over a three-day period in early March.[22]

The recommencement of the Diver campaign had therefore not started well and the rate of successful V1 interceptions had fallen. As many as one third of the V1s reached London. Matters soon improved with 125 V1s being engaged over the rest of the month when 86 were destroyed by AA fire and 13 reached the capital. In good conditions they could be detected up to about 10,000 yards in daytime and up to 25,000 yards at night when the exhaust could be more readily detected. The SCR 584 radar could detect V1s up to at least 25 miles.

The last V1s to reach London arrived on 28 March. The final ramp launches from Holland followed the next day. Twelve were plotted in the morning but only eight of them made it to the coast and all were shot down over land. The final V1 to threaten the country approached the Suffolk coast when the guns of Brigadier Rowbotham's 55 Brigade engaged and destroyed it over the sea off Orfordness at 12.43 on 29 March. Those living near the coast would no longer have their peace shattered by the gunfire and the approach of the V1s.

After a campaign lasting 290 days, the V-weapon threat was now over. Those living in Suffolk on the V1-corridor had been put at considerable risk by the Diver defence activities, but this was seen as necessary for the greater good. Norfolk and Suffolk are primarily rural counties and the reports show that most of the incidents occurred in areas of low population. The V1s that landed in built-up areas, such as the two in Ipswich, highlight the devastation that regularly occurred in London.

Although not part of the Diver Strip, the Weybourne camp on the north Norfolk coast played an important role in training the AA gun crews. Military defences were located there in the First World War with 3-inch guns on the cliffs, but it was not until 1936 that a permanent military camp began to be built and would eventually become a heavily defended area. The Royal Regiment of Artillery had several roles, one of which was to man the AA guns. In 1940, women of the ATS started training the gunners in the identification of enemy aircraft along with their speed, height and direction. The predictors would then calculate the coordinates, which were relayed to the 3.7-inch HAA guns and the 40mm LAA Bofors guns.[23]

Weybourne was one of the largest AA practice camps in the country, having the advantage that shrapnel from the shells fell into the sea. The camp closed in 1958, by which time some 1½ million shells had been fired. Around 300,000 men had been trained there on the guns between 1939 and 1945. The site is now home of the Muckleburgh Military Collection, where there is a great deal to see, including a V1 on a ramp. A visit is recommended. (www.muckleburgh.co.uk)

Notes

1. The National Archives (TNA), WO 166/16693, War Diary 57th Brigade.
2. Dobinson, C., *Operation Diver*, Historic England, 2019, p. 311.

3. Imperial War Museum, photo caption H39586.
4. TNA, WO 166/14841, War Diary 189th HAA Regiment.
5. Ibid., 2, pp. 422–428.
6. 6   Liddiard, R. and Sims, D., *A Very Dangerous Locality*, University of Hertfordshire Press, 2018, pp. 133–138.
7. Ibid., 2, p. 422.
8. Ibid., p. 334.
9. Douglas Brown, R., *East Anglia 1944*, Terence Dalton, 1992, p. 101.
10. Ibid., 2, p. 327.
11. Smith, P., *Air-launched Doodlebugs*, Pen and Sword Aviation, 2006, pp. 153, 154.
12. Routledge, N., *Anti-Aircraft Artillery 1914–55*, Brassey's, 1994, p. 424.
13. TNA, WO 166/14640, War Diary 5th HAA Brigade.
14. Ibid., 1.
15. Jennings, M., *Royal Air Force Coltishall*, Old Forge Publishing, 2007, p. 129.
16. Ibid., 6, p. 282.
17. Staff, D., May 2021.
18. Beyer Peacock and Co., *The Second World War*, 1945.
19. Ibid., 2, p. 331.
20. Ibid., 11, p. 30.
21. Ibid., 2, p. 350.
22. Ibid., p.351.
23. Savory, M., *History of the Defences of Weybourne*, 2020.

The Royal Observer Corps

The ROC, whose motto was 'Forewarned is Forearmed', played a very important role throughout the war. Its origins date back to the First World War when the Metropolitan Observation Service was formed. The Observer Corps was inaugurated in 1925 and was a civilian organisation. It came under the control of the RAF in 1929. Following the vital role played by the Corps in the Battle of Britain and the Blitz, it received Royal status in 1941.

An Observation Post would be set up on high ground to gain the best view of any aircraft in the surrounding area. Its construction was often quite basic and in many instances was not much more than a wooden enclosure with an open top to allow a clear view. Higher vantage points were used where possible, such as church towers, Martello towers at Felixstowe and the lighthouse at Pakefield. Posts were continuously manned 24 hours a day throughout the war. The main equipment provided was the plotting instrument, a table and tripod, a pair of binoculars, two torches and a direct telephone connection to the Centre.[1]

Hadleigh ROC was formed in 1929. Post J3 was located off Station Road. The roof, which would have provided some weather protection, is rolled back.

Two Observers were always present at each Post. When a V1 was seen, the first Observer estimated its height and set it on the vertical scale of the instrument plotter. The V1 was then visually located through the sighting bar. This in turn moved the sliding base mechanism to position a pointer over the Post map, from which a four-figure reference was obtained.

The second Observer wrote this reference down and telephoned it through to the ROC Centre. A headset was worn along with the microphone mounted on a breast plate which was 'on' when near the mouth and 'off' when pushed down. The message would start with Diver—Diver—Diver, followed by the Post reference, e.g.

14/E2 which was Southwold, and two numbers such as 1 at 2 which meant one V1 at 2,000 feet. Then followed the map reference and the direction of travel. As the V1 flew out of one area, it was picked up by the next Post which phoned in their data. The Plotter at the Centre was then able to estimate the height by triangulation of all the data.

The Operations Room at the Centre was blacked out except for the illumination on the tables. The Bury St Edmunds 14 Group Centre at the Guildhall had around 100 full-time staff working on three shifts every day of the year. The plotters were seated around the main plotting-table with each one being in direct contact with a cluster of Posts. Colour-coded counters were placed on the map table at the reported position of an aircraft or

Norwich ROC Centre. Each plotter at the table is in telephone contact with a cluster of Posts. On the balcony are the controllers, tellers, and other personnel who communicate with the many services involved.

V1. The colour was determined by the operations room clock which had 5-minute segments of red–yellow–blue, repeating at the start of each 15-minute period. Later in the war these segments were reduced to 2 ½ minutes.

The information displayed on the table was processed on the upper balcony level where the main personnel were the duty controller, Post controller, tellers, Inter-Group liaison, warning officer, interrogator and recorder. The tellers communicated with fighter operations rooms, and also provided information on incoming and outgoing tracks for handing over to neighbouring Groups. This information was displayed on a separate long-range-plotting-board. The interrogator liaised with GCI radar units while the warning officer operated the air raid warning system, and contacted the ARP, police, fire service, utility companies and local factories.[2]

When the Corps was re-organised in 1942, women were also enrolled. It was anticipated that this would create problems at the Posts as the two Observers would need to spend long periods together in most inhospitable conditions. Those who could cope with these conditions were found to be very good Observers. Women were not allowed to share night shifts with men. Personnel were divided into two

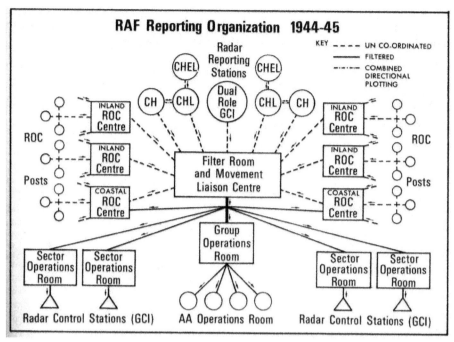

RAF Reporting Organization 1944-45

classes: A Class worked full time putting in at least 48 hours a week, B Class was part time and could work up to 24 hours a week. This fitted in well for those in reserved occupations and women who had domestic commitments. The pay was 1/3d per hour for men and 1/- per hour for women.

Felixstowe ROC had Posts on P and Q Martello towers. Observers have gathered together, with Toddy Porter and Stanley Douthwaite either side of the plotting instrument.

Some ROC Posts, such as Felixstowe, were provided with Totter equipment which enabled them to launch flares in the direction of a V1 so that fighter planes could lock onto its trail.[3]

The ROC Centres in the eastern counties during the V-weapon campaign were:

Norfolk. No. 16 Group, Fairfield, Lime Tree Road, Norwich. Controller C. F. Hill.

Suffolk. No. 14 Group, The Guildhall, Bury St Edmunds. Controller F. T. Bright.

Essex. No. 18 Group, Errington Lodge, Lexden Road, Colchester. Observer Commander D. Miller.

The Posts were formed into clusters, typically consisting of three but sometimes four Posts. The clusters were not specific to the Centres of the counties as they overlapped. There were 38 Posts in the Bury St Edmunds Centre, which also controlled Posts in Norfolk such as Thetford and Long Stratton, while Colchester Centre controlled Posts in south Suffolk such as Aldeburgh and Felixstowe.

Southwold Post, for example, telephoned information on V1 sightings directly to Bury St Edmunds Centre. Seated around the map table were 12 plotters who were each responsible for a cluster of Posts. The information provided the number of the incident in the day, the number of V1s, their height and direction. The ROC Centres and the Chain Home radar stations sent information to the Filter Room

Bury St Edmunds ROC with Percy Thompson standing behind the plotters. In the background is the long-range plotting-board that enabled tellers in neighbouring Groups to hand over tracks.

and Movement Liaison Centre. From there it was sent to the Group Operations Room, AA Operations Room/Batteries, Searchlights, Sector Operations Rooms and airfields.

It had been known since the autumn of 1943 when the first French launching sites were spotted, that attacks were to be expected. Operation 51 instructions were issued to the ROC on 22 April 1944 under the heading Detection and Reporting of Hostile Pilotless Aircraft (Code Word Diver). It was on 13 June that the first V1 was detected, not by radar but by a builder and a greengrocer with a pair of binoculars in their ROC Post on the top of a Martello tower at Dymchurch in Kent. At 04.08 they saw a long rocket shape with a red glare from the flames and with sparks pouring from the rear end, and making a noise like "a Model T Ford going up a hill".

When it was about five miles from the coast, they were certain what it was and called "Mike Two, Diver—Diver—Diver, one four, north-west, one at one".[4] When the signal was received at the air defence centre at Bentley Park it set off a chain of communications. By the end of the day, four V1s had been despatched, landing near Gravesend, Cuckfield, Sevenoaks and Bethnal Green.

The radar stations had not been able to detect the V1s due to a combination of clutter on the signals and flying too low to be detected. Only three days later, on 16 June, V1s made their first appearance in Suffolk. The Badingham ROC post (F1) detected the first one, which exploded at 00.31. The report of the incident is summarised as follows.[5]

This ROC Post report[s] the explosion of Glider type radio controlled E/ Aircraft at 00.31 hours. It approached from the East, coming North East, at approximately 3,000 feet, dropping as it approached the vicinity of the ROC to what appeared to be tree top level. Eye witness accounts, from several sources, state that it burst in the air with a heavy explosion and a subsequent minor explosion.

PC Denney, of Peasenhall, described the PAC [V1] as coming in with a flame behind and with a swishing jerky noise similar to an aircraft in distress. He then heard a loud explosion and felt the effect in the village, where damage occurred to some houses by blast to ceilings and windows. The blast extended up to approximately 1 mile.

The PAC was completely destroyed, and all fragments of casing, wire, coils, metal tubes or pipes were collected for examination.

The second V1 on that day exploded at 16.13 in a wheat field at Woolverstone, causing minor damage to property up to a mile away. 18 Group Post L2 at Earls Colne in Essex had already observed it.

There were 41 ROC Posts in Suffolk including coastal ones at Aldeburgh,

Felixstowe, Lowestoft, Orford, Pakefield and Southwold. Norfolk had around 50 Posts with coastal ones at Brancaster, Caister, Cley, Cromer, Gorleston, Hunstanton, Mundesley, Wells and Winterton. These Posts, and particularly the Suffolk ones, were on the frontline for detection of the incoming air-launched V1s. The tranquillity of the sites was regularly shattered when the AA guns of the newly formed Diver Strip went into action from September 1944.

The Aldeburgh Post 18/H1 had opened in 1936 at Gorse Hill. In 1944 their new neighbour was the No. 3 gun of Site S7, 424 Battery, 138 HAA Regiment. At 20.21 on 5 November their AA fire hit a V1 causing it to crash onto the gun site. What was most unusual was that it did not explode, but petrol from its fuel tank ignited, causing burns to five of the gunners. The warhead came off the main body and fell onto the gun-laying radar equipment. The Observers in their nearby Post saw the V1 coming towards them.[6]

> …it kept coming, and very nearly straight for us, much lower than we were perched (20 feet up). The next thing we realised it was passing underneath us practically on the ground, and its starboard wing caught one of the guns and knocked the warhead off. The rest of the bomb ploughed through the tents behind the guns, setting them all alight except one, and that one held all the ammunition, so really it was two lucky escapes in a matter of minutes.

The Observers were severely shaken by the experience and reported to the Colchester Centre that "diver 286 had passed within ten feet of their Post, with motor still running and that it had set light to the gunners' tents". Five soldiers suffered various degrees of burns and one subsequently died.[7] The Observers sought permission to evacuate the Post as there was ammunition stored nearby and the warhead had not exploded.

The role of the Observer was very demanding, particularly if located on the coast. Periods of V1 activity could be followed by days with little or nothing to report. There were though, great numbers of Allied aircraft assembling or returning from missions, along with enemy planes that could still attack coastal targets, as well as any V1s that might be heading their way. The Southwold Post saw its fair share of action and was witness to 221 V1s in the Phase 2 period. From the Post logbook the following have been determined.

Month	V1s observed	V1s destroyed	Total V1s
September	31	13	44
October	47	40	87
November	7	44	51
December	5	22	27

January	2	10	12
TOTAL	**92**	**129**	**221**

On 31 October the Post recorded that a Flying Fortress had been shot down. The local guns had engaged the aircraft as there was no IFF (Identify Friend or Foe) displayed. Five of the crew bailed out before the plane crashed at Knodishall.[8] Whenever there was known V1 activity, Posts were notified 'Divers in Operation', followed later by 'Divers Cancelled'. This could happen many times a day. October was the busiest month for Southwold, when 87 V1s were either observed, blown up, crashed or shot down by AA or fighter planes. January 1945 saw the last of the air-launched V1s, by which time the local AA guns had perfected their routine, achieving their highest score of 10 for one day on 1 January.

The Southwold gun crews would then have to wait until 16 March before seeing action again in the final days when ramp launching of the V1s was reintroduced. There was, however, still much for the ROC to record, with a large number of aircraft still passing over along with naval activity. Then it was all over and the Observers had to settle back into a routine of being home at night rather than watching the skies for V1s or enemy planes.

Captain Bright MBE, DFC, Controller of Bury St Edmunds Centre, said in a post-war speech.[9]

> But for our work there would have been no public warnings by siren, and there was no other organisation which could have given the required information to those who sounded the siren when the Doodlebugs came over; we were able to perform good service by warning everyone in front that they were coming. Many thousands of people were able to sleep safely relying on our warnings of any Doodlebug approaching…When the Germans introduced their last terror weapon, the long range rocket, the ROC reported their trails as they appeared.

Air Chief Marshal Sir Roderick Hill succinctly summed up the work of the ROC in his official report in 1948.[10] "The part played by the Royal Observer Corps—the silent service of the air defences—was an epic in itself."

The Norfolk & Suffolk Aviation Museum (www.aviationmuseum.net) has a building dedicated to the ROC. A recreation of the Bury St Edmunds ROC Centre Operations Room can be seen in its original location in The Guildhall. Visit www.burystedmundsguildhall.org.uk for event and visitor information.

Notes

1. www.roc-heritage.co.uk.
2. Ibid.
   Andy Bowles, January 2023.
3. Osbourne, M., and Graham Keer, A., *20th Century Defences in Britain, Suffolk*, Concrete Publications, 2008, p. 130.

4. Wood, D., *Attack Warning Red*, Macdonald and Jane's, 1976, p. 8.
5. The National Archives (TNA), HO 198/77, Pilotless Aircraft Reports, Region 4.
6. Dewing, G., *Aldeburgh 1939—1945*, Dewing, 1995, p. 43.
7. Ibid.
8. Bob Collis.
9. *Bury Free Press*, 11 May 1945.
10. *The London Gazette*, Supplement, 19 October 1948.

Radar

The development of radar (radio direction and ranging) played a major role in the Battle of Britain, as the range, height, direction and numbers of enemy fighter planes could be established in time for our fighters to intercept them. It would also play an important role in tracking the V1s. Suffolk was at the forefront of these developments. It was early in 1935 that Robert Watson Watt and Arnold Wilkins performed their initial experiments near Daventry, where they recorded reflected radio signals from a Heyford bomber. The success of the experiments led to substantial Government funding to develop what was known as Radio Direction Finding (RDF). The term radar was not adopted until 1942.

The need for great secrecy meant the site selected for development had to be well away from public view. Orfordness had played an important role for aviation research in the First World War and was the chosen location, with work commencing there in May 1935. The conditions were extremely basic as the site had not been used for many years and the buildings were very dilapidated. By the end of the year though, the results had been so successful that Government funding was given for the construction of five RDF stations.

It was soon found that the facilities on Orfordness were no longer adequate to keep pace with the rapid developments, and the search for an alternative site took them to Bawdsey Manor, some ten miles away as the V1 flies. This impressive building had been constructed for Sir Cuthbert Quilter, who considerably enlarged it over his lifetime. The Manor was purchased from the family in 1936 for the sum of £24,000 and became Bawdsey Research Station. Great strides were then made, which included the installation of radar in aircraft and the development of a system to identify whether they were 'friend or foe' (IFF). Pioneer work on radar application to the control of AA guns and searchlights was also carried out, which would play an important part in the Diver campaign.

The stations were called Chain Home (CH) and had four steel transmission towers in a line, 360 feet high. Each tower was built off four large concrete foundations and had cantilevered steel platforms located at 50, 200 and 350 feet above the ground. The receiving towers were of wooden construction, 240 feet high and set out in the form of a rhombus. Bawdsey Manor was handed over to the RAF in 1937 to become the world's first radio location unit.[1] The first five stations were completed in 1938, and located between Dover and Bawdsey. A further 13 stations were then added between the Isle of Wight in the south and Angus in the north. Local ones were at High Street, Darsham in Suffolk, along with Stoke Holy Cross and West Beckham in Norfolk.

The four 350-foot high steel transmitter towers of Bawdsey Chain Home station. In the background are the four 240-foot high wooden receiver towers.

There were always concerns that if war broke out, the towers would be an obvious target for enemy attack. These concerns were heightened in August 1939 when Graf Zeppelin LZ130, with scientists and radio receiving equipment on board, carried out an audacious spying mission along almost the whole east coast of England and Scotland. The Zeppelin provided the biggest echo ever seen on a CH display. When war was declared on 3 September, the evacuation plan for the Research Station was put into action, when it initially moved to Scotland. The CH station remained as RAF Bawdsey.

The aerials on the early east-coast stations were suspended between upper and lower platforms of individual towers, not between them.[2] At some point in time, modifications were made with aerial arrays being strung between towers. Peggy Butler, who was a plotter at Bawdsey in 1944, throws some light on this matter along with her close encounter with a V1.[3]

> At first I was scared, but after the night when I was about to be relieved of my PPI (Plan Position Indicator) duties, a "Diver" was approaching the station; so donning my tin hat I went outside the Ops Hut to watch it (as I thought) fly safely over the aerials and into the marshes. But as I gazed 360 feet heavenwards, the Diver roared between the number three and four aerials and shot through the trees behind me. Had it chosen aerials one and two, which had the C.H. transmitter array strung between them, I should not now be writing this book.

This indicates that in late 1944, there was a hybrid arrangement of aerials at Bawdsey. In wartime, nothing stood still for long, whether it was the location of troops, the development of weapons or technology. Chain Home stations would have adopted the latest arrangements while they were being initially constructed. The V1 that Peggy saw early on 5 September exploded without damage on King's Fleet marshes just across the river from Bawdsey. Had it been slightly to one side, the outcome would certainly have been very different.

Chain Home receiver room. A Mark 3 Console is in use on the right while on the left an operator is at an RF7 Receiver. © IWM, CH15176.

The limitation of these early systems was that they could not detect aircraft movements below about 500 feet and could only 'see' out to sea. These problems were addressed by further developments of Chain Home known as Chain Home Low (CHL), introduced in 1939, and Chain Home Extra Low (CHEL).

Bawdsey Chain Home Receiver Room. Fl Officer P Wright (to right) supervising WAAF operators Joan Lancaster, Elaine Miley, Gwen Arnold and Joyce Hollyoak who are at work on the plotting-room map. © IWM, CH15331.

These new systems performed a 360 degree scan, unlike CH which was only outward looking. These aerials at Bawdsey were located on the lower platforms of the steel towers. By the end of 1943, CH, CHL and CHEL had been completed at other stations.

The V1 was in theory the ideal target for detection by radar as it progressed at a steady speed in a straight line, unlike aircraft that were always changing direction. There was still the problem of detecting the low-flying Heinkel 111s that were air-launching V1s off the coast. In November 1944, modifications were made to radar stations at Bawdsey, Hopton, Happisburgh, Trimley St Martin, Neatishead and Greyfriars to improve the range of these stations at low level.[4]

Robert Watson Watt had put forward the theory that women would make better RDF operators than men, "alertness, keenness of perception, delicacy of touch, and, immeasurably above all else conscientiousness to a degree unattainable in the men who were likely to be available for RDF operator duties".[5] This observation was found to be the case and the work was performed mainly by women of the WAAF. Peggy Haynes (née Butler) also recalled these memories in 2006.[6]

> But there were a great many more V1s over than I had remembered, until I checked up recently in my diary. Everything had to be recorded. I mean, I got a note that on one night we were so busy that I was stuck on recording for nearly two hours, and I was quite hoarse by the time I'd finished because, as you recorded it, you had to relay the plots to the filter room, and so there was a lot more than one remembers. I can't say we were ever afraid, and if you were plotting you were too busy and, afterwards, you were so tired that you just went to sleep.

By 1944 there were many radar stations in Norfolk and Suffolk, the main ones being: Aldeburgh (Martello Tower), Bawdsey, Benacre/Covehithe, Dunwich/Greyfriars, Happisburgh, High Street/Darsham, Bard Hill/Salthouse, Hopton, Neatishead, Stoke Holy Cross, Thorpeness, Trimley St Martin, West Beckham and Winterton.

In early 1944, Mosquitos from RAF Coltishall were taking off under the control of Neatishead GCI (Ground Controlled Interception). After climbing to around 17,000 feet they were handed over to the CHL station at Happisburgh who gave them vectors for the enemy aircraft.[7] On 9 November a Coltishall Mosquito caught a Heinkel in the process of launching its V1. They were on patrol under the control of Hopton CHEL when they saw what looked like a V1 being launched about 100 miles off the coast, east of Hopton.[8]

The developments in radar, along with the use of the proximity fuse for the AA guns, transformed the success rate in downing V1s. One AA battery Commander in discussion about radar said, "When the doodle-bugs first started coming over the Brass Hats

Hopton Chain Home Low radar station opened in 1940. The transmitter aerial array is on top of the 185-foot high steel mast, while the receiver array is on the 20-foot high wooden gantry at low level next to the Operations Block. © IWM, 15183.

told you what a fine fellow you were if you managed to shoot one down. Before the end they wanted to know the reason why if you let one get away."[9]

The V2 was a very different weapon due to its far greater speed, up to 3,600 mph and downwards travel from a height of some 60 miles. A committee was set up under Sir Robert Watson-Watt to determine whether current Chain Home stations

The last Chain Home transmitter tower at Bawdsey was demolished in 2000.

would be able to track the V2. This would require highly skilled operators, along with new special equipment which was due to be in service in the summer of 1943.

It was determined that London could potentially have a four-minute warning. Certain radar stations, including Bawdsey and High Street (Darsham), were able to detect 'echoes' from the rockets on their cathode ray oscilloscopes. These would be reported to the RAF Filter Room at 11 Group HQ, who would be able to instigate the normal alert process.

Jose Rule worked at Bawdsey and recalled the procedure to detect the V2.[10]

When the V2 rockets came along we could plot these on special equipment which used the upper part of our CH lobes. This set, known as "Oswald", recorded the rocket for a few seconds as it passed through the top of our lobe. We could only watch Oswald's screen for fifteen minutes before changing operator, because the trace showed so briefly, that if you blinked it could be missed. A camera operated within Oswald recording all we had seen. As we espied our rocket we yelled "Big Ben at Bawdsey" down the line to Stanmore, who, a few minutes later instructed us to "Change Oswald". This was our cue to take out the film, insert a fresh one and then send someone to our dark room to develop the used film. From the information gained from our film and those of other CH stations, the launching site could be traced, and hopefully our bombers sent to destroy them. Londoners could have been given a four-minute warning of the approaching rocket, but I suppose the disruption over the entire area would have been too great to warrant this.

Consideration was also given to a blanket barrage of AA fire that might hopefully impact the incoming V2. General Pile had existing GL radar modified and recalibrated with a new aerial array that could detect V2s at a very long range. An experimental station was set up near Aldeburgh with the modified GL sets coupled to the re-worked No. 10 predictors. From February 1945, plots were obtained for most V2s that had been launched. The predicted impact points, following further modifications, equated to 31 per cent of the actual impact points.

Pile then pushed for the use of concentrated AA fire on the lower part of the V2 trajectory with the hope that it would create a mid-air explosion. The proposal was to be passed up to the Cabinet. Various scientific bodies had evaluated the chances of success as exceedingly low. Watson-Watt was most pessimistic with a 1 in 10,000 chance of success. The proposal was rejected.[11]

The detection of large numbers of rockets could have enabled some form of early warning to be given to the London area. However, as the number of attacks was still relatively low, no warnings would be given except to the London Transport Passenger Board to allow closure of floodgates due to the risk of flooding if tunnels were breached under the Thames.[12]

The rapid developments in RDF that took place at Orfordness and Bawdsey had a profound effect on the outcome of the Battle of Britain and everything that led from there, including the V-weapons. The Chain Home stations with their very tall transmitter towers remained a post-war feature for some years, but they are now long gone.

We are fortunate to have two excellent radar museums. Bawdsey Radar Transmitter Block (www.bawdseyradar.org) and RAF Air Defence Radar Museum Neatishead (www.radarmuseum.co.uk). There is much to see, and visits are recommended.

Notes

1. Kinsey, G., *Bawdsey, Birth of the Beam*, Terence Dalton, 1990, p. 48.
2. Latham, C., and Stobbs, A., *The Birth of British Radar, The memoirs of Arnold 'Skip' Wilkins OBE*, Radio Society of Great Britain, 2011, pp. 98–100.
   RDF Manual, Volume (1A), Issue 2, 1938 (with 1939 amendments), Part11, Chapter 1 RDF Aerial Systems.
3. Butler, P., *Searching in the Dark*, HPC Publishing, 1994, p. 120.
4. Grehan, J., *Hitler's V-Weapons, An Official History*, Frontline Books, 2020, p.157.
5. Watson-Watt, R., *Three Steps to Victory*, Odhams, 1958.
6. Heath, D., *Shout and Whisper*, Bawdsey Radar Trust, 2010, p. 55.
7. Jennings, M., *Royal Air Force Coltishall*, Old Forge Publishing, 2007, p. 112.
8. Ibid., p. 129.
9. Hallows, R., *Radar*, Chapman & Hall, 1946, p.129.
10. Hare, D., Bawdsey Radar Trust.
11. Routledge, N., *Anti-Aircraft Artillery 1914–55*, Brassey's, 1994, p. 420.
12. Ibid., 4, p. 175, 176.

Evacuees

An East Suffolk Police report of 12 July 1944 regarding V1s and evacuees noted,[1] 'A large number of people are now coming into the area from London and districts subjected to this form of bombing and, judging by their demeanour, it appears to shake morale more than bombs dropped from enemy aircraft.' Norfolk and Suffolk were no strangers to evacuees as great numbers had arrived in 1939 before war had been declared. Most had returned by Christmas that year as there had been no bombing, a period known as the 'Phoney War'. This all changed from September 1940 when towns and cities were subject to regular bombing raids, known as the Blitz, and evacuees again left for safer areas. The first raid on Norwich was even earlier, on 9 July.

However, by mid 1944 most evacuees had returned home and in the period following D-Day, there was hope that the war was going in the Allies favour. The arrival of the V1s in June had been expected and by the end of that month they had caused the death of 231 children below 16 years of age. In early August Churchill advised those classes eligible for evacuation to leave the capital "in a timely, orderly and gradual manner".[2] The first organised parties left London on 3 July. This was a grave situation and by the end of August 1944 nearly 1.5 million people had already left London.

In the Suffolk town of Framlingham, the first quota of 49 evacuees arrived there by coach from Saxmundham station on 28 July.[3] The Area School was a new building which opened in 1937 and offered good facilities including a canteen, which most schools did not have. The records show that 41 evacuees were registered for the new term in September with many of them billeted some distance from the town.[4] To reach school they were issued with bicycles. The register for the Sir Robert Hitcham Junior School in the town shows that 37 evacuees joined between July and October, their parents having decided a temporary home in the country would be safer than staying in London. They were unlikely to have known that a V1 exploded on the outskirts of Framlingham in July. In that month there were 2,453 V1 incidents in the country, falling to 1,450 in August and 87 in September.

The dates when the Framlingham children started to return home are recorded. In September, 25 per cent had returned, 17 per cent in October and 36 per cent in November. These figures were influenced by falling V1 incidents, along with the implications of Duncan Sandys announcement to the press on 7 September. There were no evacuee arrivals at the school in or after November when the official announcement of the V2 strikes had been made.

Evacuees first came to the country in 1939, but a further influx in 1944 following the V1 strikes was not received with the same enthusiasm.

The situation regarding evacuees to Ipswich had been somewhat confusing from the outset of the war. It was initially considered a safe place to send children, but the threat of invasion in 1940 changed it to a town where all non-essential people should be removed. In the next four years the Government policy did not change as the official line was that there was still risk of invasion, which in turn meant the Home Guard was retained. Those evacuees who had been sent away from Ipswich, could not return unless they were personally able to bear the cost.[5]

It was the start of the V1 campaign that would eventually unlock this situation. Ipswich was chosen as a reception area for those fleeing the new threat to life in London and the surrounding areas. This gave rise to the bizarre situation where the Government line was that Ipswich should still be evacuated, yet it wanted to send evacuees there. It took a visit from the Regional Commissioner to clarify the situation. He agreed that the original order for evacuating Ipswich could be put into 'cold storage', but it was not until February 1945 that this was formally agreed.

There were around 300 children billeted in Ipswich in the summer of 1944, but this had reduced to 163 by mid October, again reflecting the much lower number of V1 incidents in the capital at this time. About a third of the evacuees came from the London County Council who had sent two teachers to assist, but by November one of them had returned.[6]

The good folk of Norfolk and Suffolk had welcomed the evacuees back in 1939, but five years later there was not the same enthusiasm. They knew the realities of taking in evacuees, either through direct experience or the tales told by neighbours, friends and relatives. The first wave of new evacuees arrived in mid July. The small village of Peasenhall in Suffolk expected 50, but when they eventually arrived there were only 30. There were no

The Area School (now Thomas Mills High School) in Framlingham opened in 1937 and played an important role with evacuees, particularly as it had a canteen when most schools did not.

single children, mainly couples and up to five from one family. This made billeting difficult as most of the homes were small, but the people of Peasenhall 'rose nobly to the occasion.'[7] It was just as well they had not come a month earlier because Suffolk's first V1 spectacularly exploded over Peasenhall on 16 June.

Thousands arrived at Bury St Edmunds and needed to find accommodation in the town and surrounding villages. The billeting officers were under a lot of pressure, which led to Rest Centres being opened in schools and halls until permanent billets could be found. A census was undertaken to determine the housing available and the number of spare bedrooms. In the larger houses particularly, it was often recorded that more people were living there than normal, to offset the likelihood of having to take evacuees.[8]

This was a common problem and often led to heated discussions about finding suitable accommodation, with one clergyman even suggesting that if they could not put up with the hardships, they should return to London. Where there was clearly sufficient room for a household to take evacuees, those that refused were prosecuted. One Bury resident noted in her diary.[9]

> Billeting is causing much trouble in West Suffolk. People have had
> evacuees once and some say they would rather go to prison than do it
> again. Most of them cannot afford the wear and tear on furniture, linen,
> crockery, saucepans etc., as they have barely enough for themselves. And
> they haven't the surplus energy to look after additional children, or the
> desire to have their privacy invaded by persons with whom they probably
> have nothing in common. Usually, too, it means overcrowding…

As the numbers increased, so did the pressure on the authorities. It was the announcement in the press on 7 September that flying-bomb attacks should finish within a fortnight that brought a halt to the evacuation of organised parties. This in turn precipitated a return for many to their homes in London. Many of those homes had been damaged or destroyed and where this was the case people were urged to stay put until repairs had been made.

For those that did not return, there was still the risk of a damaged or errant V1 exploding nearby. And from 25 September, Norfolk and Suffolk would be on the receiving end of the new V2 rocket. Robert Lane had been sent to Norfolk to escape the V1s, but had the misfortune to be caught up in the V2 incident at Shotesham School on 6 October. His new billet was "badly messed up" and "the whole area smelt the same as after a raid during the blitz", but fortunately he was not injured.

Eileen Stringer was eight years old, and lived with her parents and younger sister Joan in Barkingside. Their world was turned upside down on 9 July 1944 when a V1 exploded nearby destroying that property and damaging many others. The roof was ripped off their house, the doors were jammed and the windows blown out. Eileen had been playing with Joan in the garden while her mother prepared food in the kitchen. They heard the sound of the V1 approaching and Eileen shouted out to her mum, "getting nearer". The sound

Eileen Stringer with her younger sister Joan. They were evacuated to Fakenham after their house in London was severely damaged by a V1 explosion.

then stopped; they all knew what that meant and dived into their Anderson shelter. That action saved them from flying glass and serious injury or worse.[10]

Despite the devastation, they stayed that night in their house, when the decision was made that mum and the two girls must be evacuated. Soon after, they boarded a train from London and later arrived at Fakenham in Norfolk. They were then taken along with many other evacuees to the local school where they were eyed up by those who were prepared to take them in. It was their good luck that they were selected by Dr Norman and his family.

Their time at Grove House turned out to be a very happy one, but they did miss their dad and grandparents. The Normans were certainly able to look after their guests. They were provided with their own large room with two single beds and a camp-bed, along with their own dining room. There was a very large garden with fruit trees, glass house and grape vines, with a gardener to look after it all. There was also a nanny who looked after the Norman's children, William and Elizabeth,

Eileen and her mother and sister were fortunate to be selected by Dr Norman to be billeted at Grove House in Fakenham. For many though, their accommodation was of a lower standard.

plus a housekeeper. The Stringers were clearly fortunate in being placed with the Norman family and stayed with them until May 1945 when they were able to return to their own house, which had by then been repaired.

The Major family from Cheam experienced a similar situation when a V1 exploded near their house. The whole family went to Norfolk, where the father, Tom, worked on an American air base near Thetford. The youngest son, John would later become Prime Minister in 1990.[11]

Norwich experienced a large intake of evacuees. In July, a decision was made to send 2,500 evacuees there, which started the process of trying to find accommodation for them. It was a difficult task, particularly when owners of the larger houses said they only had three bedrooms. These houses were needed for larger families of evacuees to prevent having to split them up. Resort was made to the use of Rest Centres and Nissen huts, the latter being most uncomfortable in very hot or cold conditions and often without mains water or electricity. Several evacuees brought little with them. The Ministry of Health provided the basic minimum, consisting of a camp bed (or pallet), two blankets and bed covering but not pillows or pillow cases. A small table, kettle, frying pan and two saucepans were supplied for cooking over a small coal fire. The billeting of evacuees in Norwich in

1944 is summarised in the following table.

Type of house	Evacuees Adult	Evacuees Children
Council houses	428	715
Cottages	145	183
Terraced houses (working class)	574	833
Medium-sized houses	109	140
Large residential houses	37	43
TOTAL	**1,293**	**1,914**

This does not include 350 evacuees who were housed in the Nissen huts or empty requisitioned properties. The low uptake in the larger houses is most evident.[12]

The experiences of the evacuees inevitably varied considerably. The Stringer family were fortunate in their billeting as were others, but it was often the luck of the draw in the availability of housing and people to take them in. The daughter of one billeting officer recalled that it was 'a thankless task.' In desperation, cottages in remote locations that had not been inhabited for years and lacked basic services, would be pressed into use. The conditions were sometimes so bad that they preferred to return home and face the risks.

A letter was sent to one billeting officer, "Did you enquire about a lamp for us? It is awfully dark and miserable here at night with only one lamp. If you can get one could you let the postman have it to bring to us if he doesn't mind and that would save us that long walk."[13]

The evacuees in 1939 had a very different outlook compared with those now arriving. The first influx was initiated through the fear of mass bombing soon after war was

Nowhere was safe in wartime. Janet Brown (left) and her siblings were traumatised when a V2 exploded nearby in the Norfolk village of Bramerton on 10 October.

ST. FAITH'S & AYLSHAM RURAL DISTRICT COUNCIL

Tudor Hall,
Rose Lane,
Norwich.

25th June, 1945.

Dear Mr Stimpson,

Government Evacuation Scheme
Return of London Evacuees - Travelling Arrangements

I enclose a copy of a letter I have to-day sent to
the householders on whom certain evacuated children
are billeted in your parish, with regard to the
children's return home on Friday next the 29th instant.
I shall be glad if you will assist the evacuees
in any way you can at their request and in particular
see that they are at the place appointed to meet the
special bus at the time stated.
Billeting forms should, of course, be recovered and
sent to me for cancellation immediately the evacuees
leave.

Yours faithfully,

Clerk and Chief Billeting
Officer.

Letter from St Faith's and Aylsham RDC regarding travel arrangements for returning evacuees, some seven weeks after the end of the war.

declared. That did not happen and many returned home soon after. By 1944, the population of London had endured the Blitz and were now witnessing the new terror weapon which could fall any time of the day or night, with the droning sound of the propulsion unit followed by that awful silence and the inevitable explosion.

Nowhere was completely safe in wartime. The V1 that fell at Whinburgh on 31 July caused extensive damage to the Manor House and 25 evacuees at Manor Farm had to be re-billeted.[14] Janet Brown was a 6-year-old evacuee when she and her siblings experienced the terror of the V2 rocket attack which hit Bramerton on 10 October. "It was terrifying. There was bits of tree, metal and smoke flying through the air and we all laid there screaming. Next thing I remember is seeing my mother, with her apron on, running as fast as she could through the smoke towards us."[15]

It was not until May 1945 that Operation Return to London was circulated to local authorities, but again that was only for those that had homes to go to. There were official documents and forms to be filled in by all those returning home. Children had to be medically examined before travel. All luggage had to be fully labelled and similarly a label had to be pinned on the coats of all adults and children so that their escorts could see where they were going. Tea was served on the train, with milk for the children.[16]

For those who had no home to return to, the wait could be much longer. Over 156,000 pre-fabricated houses (prefabs) were constructed throughout the country and were intended to have a life expectancy of ten years. There were 350 built in Norwich between 1945 and 1950.[17] In Ipswich there are still 127 Council-owned prefabs, which with modern upgrades still provide good accommodation.

Many families had no home to return to. Prefabricated houses were quickly constructed in great numbers. These prefabs were at Langley Avenue in Felixstowe.

Notes

1. Suffolk Archives (SA), A 1609, East Suffolk Police Reports.
2. Grehan, J., *Hitler's V-Weapons, An Official History*, Frontline Books, 2020, p. 325.
3. *Diss Express*, 4 August 1944.
4. Lanman Museum, Framlingham, 2011.11-43.
5. Jones, D., *Ipswich in the Second World War*, Phillimore, 2005, pp. 4–5.
6. Ibid., pp. 163–164.
7. Douglas Brown, R., *East Anglia 1944*, Terence Dalton, 1992, p. 103.
8. Ibid., p. 104.
9. Mass Observation Diary, Ref., C5271.
10. Smith, Eileen, July 2022.
11. Meeres, F., *Norfolk in the Second World War*, Phillimore, 2006, p. 89.
12. Banger, J., *Norwich at War*, Poppyland Publishing, 2003, p. 91.
13. Norfolk Record Office (NRO), PD 78/153.
14. Ibid., C/APR 1/33, Civil Defence War Diary.
15. *Britain at War*, Key Publishing, September 2018.
16. Ibid., 12, PD 78/152, Depwade RDC.
17. www.norwich.gov.uk.

V1s over Norfolk and Suffolk

The V1 campaign played out in three phases.

Phase 1. 13 June to 1 September 1944. In the first phase the V1s were predominantly land launched from ramps. These sites were then overrun by the Allies and the last ramp-launched V1 in 1944 was on 1 September. From early July, air-launched V1s were detected, with the first to land in Suffolk on 18 July.

Phase 2. 5 September to 14 January 1945. There was a lull after the first launches until they recommenced on 15 September. The V1s in this phase were all air launched from Heinkel He 111 bombers. Shortage of fuel for the planes was a major factor that eventually led to the end of this phase.

Phase 3. 3 to 29 March 1945. Ramp launches commenced from Holland with a modified V1 having an extended range of about 200 miles.

The main purpose of this book is to record the V-weapon incidents in Norfolk and Suffolk, and to also establish why they fell here. There were 93 V1 incidents in Suffolk and 13 in Norfolk. We know they were initially fired from ramps and aimed at London, but in Phase 2 there were other targets such as Portsmouth, Southampton and Manchester but none in East Anglia.

There is an enduring misconception that they were aimed at a prominent location close to where they exploded. Ipswich docks, Lowestoft and Parham airfield are such examples. Appendices I and II list the incidents in Norfolk and Suffolk, but London was their intended target. These locations are shown on Figure 10.1 for Norfolk and Figure 10.2 for Suffolk.

The first Suffolk V1 fell at Peasenhall at 00.28 hours on 16 June 1944, only three days after the start of the campaign.[1] The incident report stated that it came from the south. Further reports through to the end of August also show the direction as mainly from the south. The V1 had a compass that was preset to the target. Any deviation was detected by the gyroscopes, which caused a servo motor to adjust the control surfaces. AA fire, or fighter attack or a general malfunction could all lead to a deviation from the course to London.

The range of each missile was preset. A small propeller at the front drove a gear system which determined the number of miles travelled. When this reached the specified value, detonators were fired which caused the V1 to go into a steep dive. The intention was always for it to be under power when it hit the target, but in practice the violent movements also cut off the fuel supply, which led to the well-known 'silence' after the motor cut out, pre-empting the explosion.

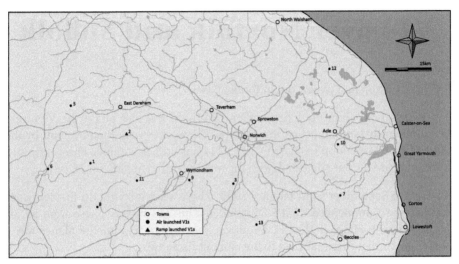

Figure 10.1. Location of V1 incidents in Norfolk.

The active Phase 1 launch sites in France were located in a zone approximately between Dieppe and the Pas de Calais. The distance to Suffolk from the central zone is similar to that for London. Therefore, if the direction of a ramp-launched V1 changed for any reason, it could well fall in Suffolk.

Norfolk was also within range of any errant V1 launched from the northern part of the zone, but too far from those in the southern area. There was only one likely ramp-launched Norfolk incident, that being on 31 July at Whinburgh. Inspector Rush of East Suffolk Police was stationed at Felixstowe and recorded that a V1 crossed the town at 03.31 travelling in a NNW direction.

The other reason why V1s landed in Norfolk and Suffolk is evident from their new direction of approach.[2] On 31 August four V1s landed: Great Wenham (from E), Capel St Mary (from NE), Raydon (from E) and Harleston, near Stowmarket (from E). The direction of approach had changed from predominantly south to either east or north-east. The V1s were now being air launched from Heinkel He 111s, operating from bases initially in France and then Holland. From the total of 106 V1 incidents in Norfolk and Suffolk, 78 per cent of them were air launched.

This new method of launch was identified on 9 July when V1s were detected approaching the Thames estuary. The direction of attack then changed, with aircraft from bases in Holland flying low over the North Sea before rising up as they approached their launch position, which could be some 40 miles from the East Anglian coast. The new launch zones meant that areas of Norfolk, Suffolk and Essex were now under the flight path of the V1. Norfolk's first air-launched V1 incident was on 10 July, with the last on 3 January 1945. The first in Suffolk was on 18 July and the last on 13 January. Mr Claxton, senior ARP warden at Fleggburgh

The sight and sound of V1s were familiar to many as they passed over on their way to London.

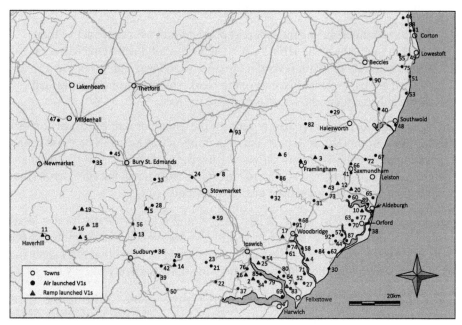

Figure 10.2. Location of V1 incidents in Suffolk.

in Norfolk, noted.[3]

> 24th September. First Flying bomb heard of in this area passed over during early morning. Reported to have exploded at Swainsthorpe.

> 9th October. Flying Bombs (apparently launched from aircraft over the North Sea) over this area just after midnight and again about 5 am.

4th November. Three Flying Bombs flying east to west passed directly over the parish. Must have travelled far inland as no explosion heard.

9th November. One Flying Bomb flying south to north passed directly over the village. Evidently this one had been misdirected or turned off course. I remember it fell in the sea well south of Haisbro [major sand bank off Norfolk coast]. Other flying bombs sailing east to west passed well inland, no explosions heard.

The 9 November incident suggests a major malfunction as it was travelling in the opposite direction to that intended. There was a high failure rate of these air-launched weapons. On 16 September, 15 planes set off with their deadly cargo fixed below their wings, but only nine were able to successfully release them, five of which were shot down and two reached London. Between a quarter and a half of all launches ended in failure.[4]

The months of October and November saw the greatest activity in Phase 2. The base log for the 390th Bomb Group at Parham noted for November.[5]

The Buzz-Bombs during the first part of the month were more active than ever. On the night of the 10th, 16 of them were shot down in the flak area east of here. On the 14th several more were shot down and two of them crashed almost together just east of the Field. The blast from them was felt by the enlisted men who were spotting on the roof.

The East Suffolk Police prepared reports for the Chief Constable to assist him with his Monthly Appreciation Report. For September it was noted, 'There has been a certain amount of Flying Bomb activity during the past month. The approach and passing over of these bombs appear to have had a more terrifying effect upon some people than bombs dropped from ordinary aircraft'.

In October, the report noted, 'The Flying Bomb attacks, although on a lesser scale [than Phase 1], are not lightly regarded—the immense possibilities of this type of weapon are realised. The public are relieved to learn that the enemy has now to use aircraft for the purpose of launching these weapons'.[6]

The appendices list the V1 incidents where many are noted as being due to AA fire as recorded in the original reports. There may well have been others where such information was unknown. The AA guns were not supposed to fire *over* towns, as a damaged V1 was always a significant threat to coastal dwellings and further inland. On 14 October at 20.00, a V1 exploded over Southwold after being hit by fire from the guns on the Common. Tom King's ARP diary noted.

Had a warning at 19.53 when I was on duty. It was fairly quiet at first then all the guns opened up on a Fly heading straight for the town there was a hell of a din, I looked outside, just as I got there a shell hit on the Fly, there was a terrific flash of orange flame followed by a hell of an explosion, glass fell everywhere, about 300 houses, 57 shops, the Church and 2 Chapels were damaged, fortunately only one person a Soldier was slightly hurt by shrapnel. There is a hell of a mess in the town, it was good shooting by the Heavy and Light AA.

Other reports show variations in the number of properties damaged. One stated that '6 members of the Home Guard assisted from 00.01 to dawn on 15 October to prevent looting.'[7]

Another report which refers to a V1 being hit by AA fire is from Orford Police to Superintendent Boreham.[8]

I beg to inform that on the morning of Saturday 11th November 44 a F.L.Y. bomb was travelling from an East to West direction when it was hit by A.A. Fire. The engine stopped, but the bomb carried on for a further 2 miles, finally hitting the ground where it exploded in a wood known locally as Brickelsea Wood.

The Government had warned about the threat of flying bombs, but the press was not allowed to give any details about the location of impacts. The accuracy of the V1 was unknown to the enemy and specific information on where they landed would have greatly assisted them. The inhabitants of Ipswich were painfully aware when their first V1 fell, on Maryon Road on 1 September, but the *EADT* could only report, 'A flying bomb which crashed on an estate on the outskirts of a town killed an airman and injured a number of people who were in bed. It was the first flying bomb to land on this town.' The reality was that it exploded at 02.18 when most would have been in bed. One man died, five went to hospital, 27 were injured, four buildings demolished and four seriously damaged.

The last ramp-launched V1s from France in 1944 were on 1 September, with two falling in Suffolk, the other being at Freston. The Maryon Road report[9] states that it was travelling from the south-east direction, indicating it to be a ramp launch.

Halton Crescent in Ipswich looking towards Campbell Road after the V1 incident on 18 October 1944 that caused loss of life and the destruction of houses.

The same view in 2023.

This incident highlights the inaccuracy of the V1, although aimed at London; it somehow found its way to Suffolk. From now on, in Phase 2, the V1s were only launched in the hours of darkness.

A similar *EADT* report on 20 October referred to 'a housing estate…in a town.' This was the 18 October incident at Halton Crescent in Ipswich, when four people were killed and many injured. The air raid RED warning was given at 23.12, with the impact at 23.27. The V1 hit the Anderson shelters of Nos. 3 and 5 which were constructed next to each other under the same earth covering. The house at No. 5 was unoccupied, but three of the occupants of No. 3 were killed. A two-month-old baby from No. 7 also died. This was the worst V1 incident for loss of life in Suffolk. Ipswich was no stranger to bombing and there was a well-rehearsed Civil Defence procedure that went into action. The report of the incident is in Appendix IX and provides a full account of all that happened.[10]

This V1 came from the north-east direction and was air launched by a Heinkel over the North Sea. There were AA guns in the vicinity, with one located near Foxhall Heath and one near the middle of the present Ransomes Europark. The diary of 16-year-old Kenneth Boynes provides an important source of information on wartime events in Ipswich at this time.[11] It includes specific details of events around Ipswich which he saw, heard or was told about. The diary tells us that it was not these local guns that were responsible for bringing down the V1 on Halton Crescent.

> Heavy AA fire was heard and numerous flashes observed as a wave of
> Flying Bombs crossed the East coast. One of the missiles was 'winged' as it
> crossed the coast, lost height rapidly as it passed across the Heath towards
> Ipswich. When only a few feet from the ground, with its motor still running
> it struck a house in Halton Crescent.

His note refers to the motor running when it impacted, although this is not mentioned in official reports. It was a tragic coincidence that these two incidents occurred within about a third of a mile of each other. Information in Kenneth Boynes's diary shows fair correlation with recorded incidents near Ipswich when he named the locations. Some entries suggest there were more blown up than are recorded in the official reports He often refers to the numbers approaching the Ipswich area and associated explosions following AA fire.

Official data on events provide the raw information. They cannot convey the anxiety of those living under the flight path of the V1. Ipswich was the largest town in Suffolk and very much on the V1s' course to London. The population heard them passing over in the dark on a regular basis. In October, for example, there were V1 incidents in the country on 22 days of the month. On the other days there was no activity, all leading to anxiety over the uncertainty of what might happen. There are few surviving log books for the ARP that provide information on the numbers passing over their area. The log for the Framsden beat of Grundisburgh ARP does survive.[12] A snapshot between 11 and 29 October 1944 shows that 26 V1s passed through the area unhindered, and that location is to the west of the main path.

Tom King's Southwold ARP diary records many V1 incidents. The following covers a small selection of those he observed.

1 July, '…I heard a noise like a Traction engine from a plane, I at once thought it was a Fly Bomb, out at sea I could see a small plane going along about 2000 ft. up and flying north…It landed in the sea east of Kessingland…This is the first Fly Bomb we have had pass the town, I hope we don't get any more…'.

19 September, 'Had a warning at 01.29 and a few minutes later heard a Fly Bomb coming in from the sea, had a look out of the front door and saw one going in just to north of the town, you could see a bright white light underneath, and a red glow from the jet propulsion unit, it was travelling very fast. Heard some more come in just south of the town, and at 01.58 heard another come in fast with its light showing, it shot over at terrific speed, and made a hell of a noise.'

23 September, 'The Coastguards told me they had seen 6 Flying Bombs go in and that ships at sea had opened fire on them.'

29 September, '…heard a Fly come in south of the town, it passed over

V1 passing over Parham airfield in late 1944. This rare image combines the V1, the searchlight beams and tracer fire from Bofors guns on the coast with the outline of Flying Fortresses.

the harbour, a few seconds later another came in low just north of the town, it passed over Reydon and all the guns north opened up, but the Fly sailed on, they were firing at the Fly, but the speed of the Fly outpaced the shells, but it was very exciting to see them fire at it.'

17 October, 'I saw 3 Fly Bombs brought down by AA, these gunners are hotstuff, also saw one of the Flying Bombs launched from a plane, and saw what I believe was a plane shot down by one of our fighters. The Fly Bombs I saw were 2 to south and 1 off the end of the pier, I saw the Fly and then saw the shell from a heavy AA gun hit

Major Price and Captain Williams from the 390th Bomb Group at Parham pose with the remains of a V1 that exploded nearby.

it, the explosion was terrific, a great orange flash and then falling pieces, amazing sight…'.

6 November, '…8 Flying Bombs went past the town and 6 were shot down by gunfire, I saw 5 of them explode…The searchlight at Easton came up several times, one Fly crashed on land in the Minsmere area after having its tail shot off.'

Data for the air-launched Phase 2 (5 September to 14 January 1945)[13] show that approximately 410 V1s crossed the East Anglian coast line. Of that number, 66 landed in Suffolk and 11 in Norfolk, while the remainder carried on towards other counties and the capital. Along with the additional incidents in Phases 1 and 3, this shows that the dreaded sound of the V1 would have been all too familiar to those who lived near or under the flight-path to London. The base history for Parham airfield even noted,[14] '…many passed over the 390th base. Some were hit by coastal anti-aircraft fire and exploded. Others were deflected and landed nearby. It was common to be driven to the revetments several times in the course of a night.'

Further information is provided on some specific incidents:

21 September, near Alderton, just over two miles from Bawdsey Chain Home station. A V1 exploded on the beach, which in turn set off 57 beach mines. A

On returning home from the cinema, Lew and Amy Paul found their home in Carlton Colville had been destroyed by a V1. The incident on 19 November 1944 killed their two neighbours, injured many and caused much damage.

useful start to the mine-clearance programme!

12 October, 23.55, Stratford St Andrew. Major explosion just avoided when a V1 landed about 250 yards from the USAAF bomb dump at Parham airfield. It hit the ground 'with engine still running'. The base history noted[15] 'Base personnel had their biggest thrill from a fly bomb the night one was deflected by flak guns from nearby Saxmundham. It came down in a field near the station bomb dump. The blast tore down a fence and blew turf over rows of bombs, but none exploded'.

14 October, 20.14, Lowestoft. V1 hit by AA fire exploded in the inner harbour. Damage to Brooke Marine, the Silk Factory, British Petroleum, LNER railway and some 255 properties.

14 October, 20.25, Hopton, near Corton. V1 damaged by AA fire landed but failed to explode. The next day one officer was decapitated and another wounded following an explosion while inspecting the fuse and detonator. They were from a Bomb Disposal Squad based in Thorpeness.

14 November, 19.14, Martlesham. V1 came in low with 'engine off', hit trees and exploded within the perimeter of the aerodrome. Damage caused to Nissen huts and 30 houses up to half a mile from impact, where men were billeted. Two men were seriously injured and two slightly.

SECRET.

EAST SUFFOLK POLICE—DAILY SITUATION REPORT.

Form No. 85.
Rcd – 1145 Sheet No. 1.

Station FRAMLINGHAM

Signature, Rank and No. .... A. Moon Sergeant.

Time of attack White 1159 hrs.

Date Wednesday, 19th July, 1944.

A. Bomb No. and Time.	B. Size of crater.	C. Nature of Soil.	D. Size of Bomb.	E. Parish.	F. Grid No.	G. Damage, etc. (To include distance from centre of crater.	H. Killed.		Casualties.			
							M.	F.	C.	M.	F.	C.
Ex FLY hrs 1145	2' x 4'	Wheat Field. Clay.	'FLY'	DENNINGTON. about 300 yards north east Framlingham Hall.	732843	Blast damage to growing wheat approximately 2 acres. Damage to roof & windows at Framlingham Hall, roof damage to farm buildings owned and occupied by Mrs Charlotte Garrard, 300 yards south west of crater. Roof damage to Dairy Farm House & farm buildings owned by Mrs Garrard and occupied by George Nurse. 500 yards south west of crater. Roof damage and windows broken at Hall Cottage, occupied by Walter Tye. 250 yards south west of crater.	–	–	–	–	–	–

The incident sheet for the V1 that passed over Framlingham and exploded near Dennington on 19 July 1944.

19 November, 19.57, Carlton Colville. V1 hit by AA fire and exploded in farm yard. Two cottages were destroyed. Farm buildings, a bungalow and five houses were damaged. Minor damage to over 100 more houses. Two women killed and 17 people injured. The occupants of one of the houses had been to the cinema that evening. On their return, they found their home was destroyed and their neighbours had been killed. Propaganda information was found from the V1 titled *The Aftermath No. 6*. The leaflets contained photographs of alleged Russian atrocities in Germany.[16]

13 January 1945, 06.05, Capel St Andrew. V1 hit by AA fire landed near the front door of Capel Green Farm but did not explode. The Gladwin family quickly evacuated the area. When the Bomb Disposal Squad arrived, they found the V1 buried in deep mud. They had instructions to X-Ray the bomb to determine the type of fuse and to see if there were any attachments or 'booby traps'. Standing almost up to their waists in mud, checking the fuses became a very difficult and dangerous process. They decided the bomb had to be removed from the mud, so a tractor was requested from RAF Woodbridge. Some hours passed before it arrived with a steel cable which was passed around a tree and attached to the bomb. It could not be moved. It was decided, at great risk, to give it a quick tug but then the cable broke. A heavier cable finally saw the bomb extricated from the mud. The V1 was found to be in such good condition that it was sent to America.[17] This was the last air-launched V1 incident in Suffolk. Phase 2 came to an end the next day.

By March there had been several weeks with no V1 activity, primarily due to fuel supply problems for the aircraft. It was likely a relief to the German aircrew who often flew two sorties a night and occasionally three. There was no actual shortage of V1s as they were still being ramp launched at targets on the continent. The Germans still held much of Holland and had also developed a longer-range ramp-launched V1.

The incident reports provide factual information on incidents but lack the general comments on the daily perception of the V1s. Boynes's diary started on 3 September 1939 and provided regular entries for anything significant that affected Ipswich through to the final day of the war. There is evidence here to indicate that there were AA guns active in the Ipswich area, see 12 October. Many of the entries were quite similar and the following represent typical examples from the time of V1 activity.

Chelmondiston Church after the V1 incident on 10 December 1944. One person was killed, several injured and buildings demolished or damaged.

16 June. Something was seen in sky to the south of Ipswich. Almost immediately afterwards a very heavy explosion was heard and a column of smoke was seen rising from the area of Woolverstone Park. [This was the second V1 in Suffolk, the first arriving earlier the same day at Peasenhall].

18 July. A flying bomb passed right over Ipswich at about 1,500 feet. Some minutes later a very heavy explosion was heard as it came down in Gipping Wood at Stowupland.

Mancroft Towers in Oulton Broad was severely damaged when a V1 exploded in nearby trees on 19 October 1944.

5 September. Continuous stream of about 30 doodlebugs came over E. Anglian coast, 3 extremely heavy explosions were heard as some of the missiles came down near Ipswich. About 6 robots were visible in Ipswich.

23 September. Heavy anti-aircraft fire was heard as more flying bombs came over E England.

Personnel from the 452nd Bomb Group at Deopham Green inspect the remains of a V1 that exploded close to the base on 3 January 1945.

After the war, USAAF Great Ashfield was taken over by Maintenance Units of the RAF as a sub-site for bomb storage. The photo shows parts of several unused V1s that were stored there.

Those passing over Ipswich were much higher than usual.

29 September. Searchlights and guns went into action as 3 flying bombs approached Ipswich… One came directly over the centre of the town missing the roof-tops by only a few feet.

12 October. AA guns opened fire on a robot caught in the searchlights over Ipswich.

21 October. Many flashes and explosions indicated that several flying bombs had been hit by the terrific AA barrage put up by our guns on the coast… One explosion shook Ipswich a few seconds after a robot was blown up in mid air.

4 November. Heavy gunfire was heard and explosions shook Ipswich, as Heinkel carriers launched more flying bombs…

10 November. The most flying bombs in the area of Ipswich yet. At least 19 came very near the town and 14 of them were blown up. Heavy explosions followed their destruction by anti-aircraft fire. One robot came down on the Woodbridge by-pass between Melton and Ufford and another near Mendlesham.

13 November. A flying bomb passed over Ipswich at a very low altitude. Searchlights and AA guns were in action and some minutes later a bright flash was seen and an explosion followed…

23 November. Heavy gunfire was heard as flying bombs came over E. Anglia. One which came down between Holbrook, Freston and Wherstead shook Ipswich with a great explosion. [Incident report states Wherstead.]

24 November. Ten flying bombs crossed the East Coast. 9 were hit by our guns

and the remaining one passed over the centre of Ipswich at a tremendous height. Cutting out just beyond the town it came down at Polstead.

9 December. Flying bomb attacks resume after a lull of several days.

12 December. 3 heavy explosions followed the passing of 3 flying bombs over Ipswich. Searchlights and AA guns were in action as other robots crossed the coast.

3 March. Flying bombs over here for the first time in several weeks. [Start of Phase 3 with ramp launch from Holland.]

18 March. Gunfire heard as a buzz-bomb passed directly over the town at practically roof-top level.

27 March. Distant gunfire as buzz bombs approached the East Coast.

2 May. An announcement was issued by the Ministry of Home Security to the effect that 'The air raid warning system throughout the country has been discontinued as no more raids are thought possible...'

Although the air-launched element of the campaign fizzled out on 14 January, the V1 was still was having a devastating effect on the continent. The concern was that ramp launching would be re-introduced from sites in Holland with the modified longer-range V1, which turned out to be the case.

Phase 3 of the V1 attacks started on 3 March 1945 but it was a far less ambitious effort compared with the previous ones and only lasted just under four weeks. The Diver defence did not start well, with three Allied planes lost to AA fire in early March. Also, the rate of successful V1 interceptions had fallen, with as many as one-third of them reaching London. Matters soon improved with 125 V1s being engaged over the rest of the month, when 86 were destroyed by AA fire and 13 reached the capital.

The last V1s to reach London were on 28 March. The final ramp launches from Holland followed the next day. Twelve were plotted in the morning but only eight of them made it to the coast and all were shot down over land. The final V1 to threaten the country approached the Suffolk coast when 55 Brigade's guns engaged and it was destroyed over the sea off Orfordness at 12.43. The V-weapon threat was now over and those living near the coast would no longer have their peace shattered by the roar of gunfire.

Between June 1944 and March 1945, the two counties were subjected to the following numbers of V1 incidents.

	June	July	Aug.	Sept.	Oct.	Nov.	Dec.	Jan.	Feb.	March
Norfolk	0	2	0	1	4	2	1	3	0	0
Suffolk	4	9	11	12	27	15	9	5	0	1

The estimated number of civilians killed in England by V1s was 6,184 and 17,981 seriously injured.[18] This puts it in perspective with the 11 people killed in Suffolk.

Lieutenant Ivan Cobbold was chairman of the Cobbold brewing company in Ipswich, and founder of Ipswich Town Football Club. He came from a military background and was Commanding Officer of the Scots Greys and also liaison officer to the Supreme Headquarters Allied Expeditionary Force (SHAEF) commanded by Dwight D. Eisenhower. In the first month of the Phase 1 attacks, on 18 June 1944, Cobbold attended a service in the Guards Chapel in Birdcage Walk in London, to give thanks for the success of the D-Day landings. At 11.20 the chapel was struck by a V1. The explosion and collapse of the structure killed 121 soldiers and civilians, and seriously injured another 141. This was the single worst loss of life from a V1 in this country and Ivan Cobbold was one of those killed.

Notes

1. Suffolk Archives (SA), A 1608-3, Enemy Bombs in East Suffolk, 1943 to 1945. The National Archives (TNA), HO 198/77, Pilotless Aircraft Reports.
2. Ibid., 1, SA.
3. Norfolk Record Office (NRO), PD 82/44, Fleggburgh ARP log.
4. Zaloga, S., *German V-Weapon Sites 1943–1945*. Osprey Publishing, 2008, p. 50.
5. Parham Airfield Museum, Flying Control Historical Report for November 1944.
6. SA, A1609, East Suffolk Monthly Police Reports.
7. TNA, WO 166/14537, 54th Division War Diary.
8. SA, A 1608/1, Daily Situation reports 1944.
9. SA, DC 8/2/4/2, Ipswich Borough Air Raid Reports.
10. SA, HD 862-3, Ipswich Air Raids 1940–1945.
11. SA, HD 3071, Diary of K. W. Boynes.
12. SA, E 32/A12/1, Grundisburgh ARP Warden Book.
13. TNA, AIR 20/3684, 3685, Flying Bomb Attacks: Summary.
14. The Men and Officers of the 390th Bombardment Group, *The Story of the 390th Bombardment Group (H)*, 1947, p. 80.
15. Ibid.
16. Collis, B., and Baker, S., *The Air War over Lowestoft 1939–1945*, Lowestoft Aviation Society, 2019, p. 63.
17. Kinsey, G., *Aviation, Flight over the Eastern Counties since 1937*, Terence Dalton, 1977, pp. 99, 100.
18. O'Brien, T., *History of the Second World War; Civil Defence*, HMSO and Longmans, Green, 1955, Appendix II.

Voices of the V1

In October 2022 the author placed a letter in the *East Anglian Daily Times* seeking any recollections of V1 incidents. The response was far greater than expected. The many people who made contact were of course very young at the time but their memories were clear. In many cases it has been possible to provide a date for the incident. A selection of these recollections, all from 1944, follows.

16 June at 16.13, Woolverstone. Michael Jillings was nearly 5 years old when he witnessed the second V1 to land in Suffolk.

> We heard a noise which was getting louder; looking up we then saw this flying object in the sky with a flame coming from the rear. It flew right over us, and then the flame went out and the noise stopped, then it crashed 1,000/1,500yards away from us with a big bang, and the earth shook. We all screamed; mothers came screaming to see if we were all ok. Sometime later a fire tender turned up and the army. The site was guarded, so I don't think anyone was allowed to see the remains.

> A baby in a pram outside a nearby house was fortunate to be shielded from the blast by a brick potting shed, but ceilings in the houses came down and tiles came off the roofs.

7 July at 13.01, Worlingworth. Whenever a V1 passed low over a village or exploded nearby, it was a major event and talked about by everyone. Russell Ruffles saw the V1 coming low over Earl Soham village hall. He was in the cemetery watching someone digging a grave. Nearby in the school playground, Gordon Stannard also saw it pass over and was relieved that the motor was still running. Its unplanned destination was in a field of horse beans in Worlingworth. Minor damage was caused to eight properties. In the nearby school, the children were eating their lunch when they heard the V1 approaching, followed by a massive explosion. Gerald Hawes recalled that they were all covered with prunes and custard as the explosion lifted the tables off the floor. The headmaster, Mr Piper, then told them rather belatedly to get under the tables.

19 July just before 12.00, Kettleburgh. Mary Cracknell was in the garden at Kettleburgh School when the V1 came over. They had been told that if they were outside in the playground, they must take shelter next to the fence. Mary and her class were gardening nearby and not able to reach the fence in time, which made their teacher angry. Mary was terrified. The V1 was heading in the Framlingham direction, where Bill Flemming's father called him into the garden to witness its noisy passage over the town.

A posed photo of a family entering their earth-covered Anderson shelter.

College Road in Framlingham was no stranger to enemy activity. On 6 October 1940, eight bombs were dropped causing the death of a school teacher and much damage to property. Not far away, young Stephen Sullivan's mother stood over his high chair to protect him from the flying glass and debris. Stephen recalled the later passage of the V1 in 1944.

> I remember sitting under the table at 57 College Road when 'Auntie', Miss Banthorpe from across the road, was invited to join us. The doodlebug made a very sharp metallic clackety-clack noise. As it went over the house Auntie and my mother began to shake with fear. Auntie had very loose dentures which began to rattle in unison with the doodle bug. It was no laughing matter at the time but it still makes me smile at the memory, even now.

29 July at 01.37, Long Melford. Alan Beevis was 4 years old at the time and fast asleep along with his sister and cousin in their bedroom when the house in Liston Lane was shaken by the passage of a low-flying V1. It was a very frightening experience and one which he would never forget. The V1 exploded in a field near Bassetts Farm, just under two miles from their house, but this was unknown to him until now.

18 August at 07.24, Rosary Farm, Great Bealings. Bernard Mills lived in the California area of Ipswich, and was getting ready for school when he heard the sound of a V1. He rushed into the garden and saw it making its way in a northerly

direction across Ipswich. He was convinced it was going to hit Seckford Hall. Fortunately it fell in a wooded area in Bealings. The motor was still running when it hit the ground.

1 September at 02.18, Maryon Road, Ipswich. Bob Hoggar lived with his parents in Nacton Road, opposite the Golden Hind pub at the end of Maryon Road. They heard the siren and were quickly making their way to the Anderson shelter in their back garden when the V1 exploded in the road next to the bungalows in Maryon Road and Maybury Road. An RAF Flt Sgt billeted in No. 54 Maryon Road was killed and a further 34 people suffered injuries. Fortunately the Hoggar's house shielded them from the worst of the blast but they were still blown into their shelter.

16 October at 04.58, Trimley St Mary. David Chaplin was 4 years old when a V1 caused much damage to the cottage where he was living with his mother and aunt. They were sleeping in the next bedroom when the plaster ceiling crashed down in one large lump and broken glass was strewn everywhere. On entering David's room all they could see were his eyes amongst all the dust and debris. He called out "naughty old Germans". As it was still dark they all crawled back into bed and awaited daylight.

18 October at 23.27, Halton Crescent, Ipswich. Ken Wright was 12 years old at the time and living with his parents and six siblings in No. 15 at the end of the Halton Crescent. They heard the air raid siren, quickly dressed and all nine of them rapidly made it to their Anderson shelter in the back garden. The V1 hit the rear of No. 5, which was destroyed along with Nos. 3, 7 and 9. They had to stay in the shelter until the all-clear siren sounded at 23.46. Ken recalled that all their windows were blown out and they could not return to their home. The Salvation Army was quickly on the scene, and they all went to Holywells mansion where they were provided with straw-filled mattresses in the basement and stayed there for three days.

Mrs Wilson normally lived with her husband and daughter Carol at No. 5 Halton Crescent, but as her husband was away in the army she was staying with her mother at Over Stoke. He was due home on leave and she was to return to No. 5. Ken Wright's mother suggested his sister Doreen might like to stay with her and keep her company until her husband arrived home. Fortunately his leave was cancelled so neither Mrs Wilson nor Doreen went to No. 5, which was completely destroyed in the incident. A message that had been received with great disappointment was now responsible for saving their lives.

Pearl Wright was 6 years old and lived in Campbell Road which joins Halton Crescent. They had only just got into their air raid shelter when there was a massive explosion followed by piles of earth coming in.

Frank Rowe was ten years old when this Smyth seed drill was damaged by the V1 that exploded at Rubblestone Farm, Kelsale, on 6 November 1944.

6 November at 20.35, Kelsale. Frank Rowe's father had been drilling beans earlier that day at Rubblestone Farm. Frank, who was ten years old, was getting ready for bed when the V1 exploded about 400 yards from the house. Their Smyth seed drill was damaged yet survives to this day, but the harrows were blown up. The family was perhaps lucky as the only other misfortune they suffered that day was that their windows were bowed in and his father's hat blown off! The RAF came to inspect the damage the next day. Parts of the pulse jet and a wing spar are in the Norfolk & Suffolk Aviation Museum.

10 December at 18.50, Chelmondiston. Michael Usher was getting ready for bed when he heard the air raid siren. They had an indoor Morrison shelter but that was not big enough to take all seven of them. Soon after, he heard the roar of a V1 passing low near their cottage causing the staircase to shake. Soon after, there was a large explosion. Their cottage was fortunately not damaged, being shielded by the church. John and Elsie Rands lived in Myrtle Cottage which took a direct hit and was completely destroyed. John was outside the cottage at the time and was killed. His legs were found on the roof of a cottage. Elsie had been sitting in her armchair and both were blown into the churchyard. There were four casualties, including Elsie, requiring hospital admission, and another 17 with light injuries.

This V1 caused much damage. In addition to the demolition of Myrtle Cottage,

Nos. 1 and 2 Hill Crest and Church Cottages were so badly damaged they would need to be demolished. Another 19 buildings, including Saint Andrew's church, suffered severe damage but were assessed as repairable, while a further 60 had minor damage. The church was rebuilt and consecrated in 1957.

Morrison table shelter. Debach Airfield Museum.

12 December at 19.49, Fressingfield. A V1 that had been damaged by AA fire passed over Grove Farm where 5-year-old David Oliver was living. He heard the motor cut out, soon followed by the explosion. The windows were blown in and holes made in the walls. It landed in a field at Elm Lodge where Tommy Webster lived. The Lodge was damaged along with nearby houses and a bungalow.

Peter Watkins lives in Haverhill, but as a 6 year old he was then in Kent, the centre of Doodlebug Alley at the peak period of the ramp-launched V1s. He recalled that they would sometimes come over about six at a time. He witnessed one being tipped over by one of our fighters, which then crashed and blew up in a field near him.

Margaret Moore lived in Landseer Road, Ipswich and regularly saw V1s passing overhead while heading for the shelter. She clearly recalled the red flames coming out of the motor and how they would sometimes stop and then restart. In the 1960s, she moved to Maryon Road, the location of the first V1 incident in Ipswich.

A service held in the ruins of Chelmondiston Church. It was later rebuilt and consecrated in 1957.

Ray Beales was living in Holton near Halesworth and was familiar with the sights and sounds from the nearby American air base. The noise and flames from V1s were also common as they were air launched across the coast. One night while on his way to the shelter in his pyjamas, his father shouted out to one of them, "keep going you bugger!"

Douglas Harper was returning home with his parents one dark evening when, at the junction of Valley Road and Westerfield Road in Ipswich, they heard the characteristic sound of a German bomber. It was followed by the spluttering noise of a V1 starting and they could see the cigarette-end flame from the back. The bomber disappeared and the V1 continued in a westerly direction until out of sight. Douglas had seen several V1s flying over Ipswich and knew the sight and sound of them well. He is very certain of what he saw that evening. It is generally understood that V1s were launched over the sea several miles from the coast. It is perhaps conceivable that some problem led to one of these Heinkels being over Ipswich. We know that a Junkers aircraft landed at RAF Woodbridge by mistake in July 1944.

Gerald Hawes, of the prunes and custard incident in Worlingworth, would regularly see V1s approaching from the coast. On one night, he estimated there were around 20 of them. Although all were aimed at London, AA damage or general malfunction could see them veer off in different directions. Several incidents were recorded in Hertford, Bedford, Cambridge and the Isle of Ely. These could have been either overshoots from the early ramp-launched V1s, or the later air-launched ones which would have been visible over Suffolk.

V2s over Norfolk and Suffolk

The threat of Hitler's vengeance weapons had been known for some time but it initially was not clear what form they would take or that in fact there were two main types that were very different. Churchill had warned Parliament in February 1944 about the potential for long-range rocket attacks as well as flying bombs. By the end of July the War Cabinet had been advised that 1,000 rockets with a range of 200 miles were in an advanced state of preparation.

Following the bombing raids on Peenemunde, production of the V2 had been transferred to underground tunnels in the Harz Mountains near Nordhausen, and from January 1944 slave labour from the Dora camp was mercilessly used to manufacture them. The missiles would all be fired from mobile launchers to aid concealment from aerial reconnaissance. It was the dawn of this new form of warfare that had not been fully tested and consequently there were endless problems, with many of the rockets disintegrating or exploding on the site or soon after launch. They would turn out to be as great a danger to the launch party and anyone en route to the target, as the intended victims.

The V2 could reach an altitude of 60 miles with a speed up to 3,600 mph, reducing to less than 2,500 mph nearer impact. This new vengeance weapon did not give any warning of its approach. The first sound heard was the detonation of the warhead when it hit the ground, followed shortly after by the sonic boom. Most V2 strikes are recorded as having a double boom. Vapour trails from the ascending rockets were often observed in this country. Mick Muttitt recalled that on a school outing by horse and wagon to Dunwich, they had to keep to the cliffs as the beaches were mined. He saw a number of these vapour trails which appeared golden in colour with the sun shining through them.[1] Southwold ROC recorded the times of a great number of these launch trails, with the information being passed to the Centre. Tom King also noted.

> 26 November, 'Anglers on the Pier saw Rockets the Germans sent against this Country going up in the air…When they saw them there is a streak of light, followed by a vapour trail.'

The track of a V2 recorded in a photo taken from a Flying Fortress.

23 December, 'I looked out of the bedroom window and saw

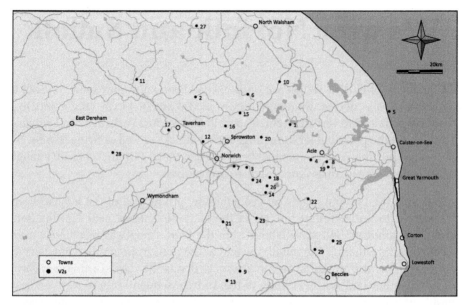

Figure 12.1. Location of V2 incidents in Norfolk.

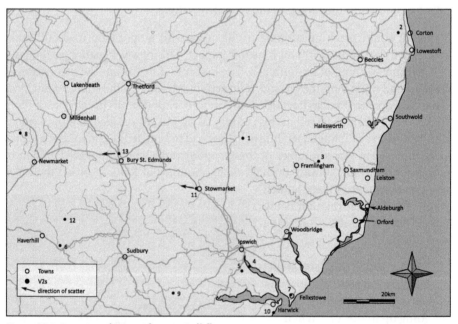

Figure 12.2. Location of V2 incidents in Suffolk.

a Rocket, one of the V2 go up in the sky from Holland, at first I thought it was Fly Bomb but saw trail of smoke behind and called Beattie [his wife] to see it.'

29 December, 'Saw some V2 Rockets go up at 09.00.'

1 January, 'See more Rockets go up just before 09.00.'

Each of these missiles had a lengthy procedure to make it ready for launch, usually lasting four to six hours. Its journey to England took only about five minutes. The first V2 rocket exploded at Chiswick on 8 September. The scale of ongoing attacks was limited by the supply of liquid oxygen for them, with a total of 26 launches up to 18 September. The airborne landings of Allied troops at Arnhem on 17 September also coincided with the movement of the launch Batteries to the east.

The V2 could take up to six hours to prepare for launch, whereas its journey to England was around five minutes. The speed before impact was about 2,500 mph.

Batterie 444 had a brief stay on the island of Walcheren in the Scheldt estuary, when their rockets were launched against London, but they were forced to move due to the advancing Allied troops. The Batterie then moved to Rijsterbos, a wooded area in south-west Friesland. This site was out of range for London so attention turned to East Anglia, with Ipswich (target 0205) and Norwich (target 0204) being selected. The only V2 specifically aimed at Ipswich by Batterie 444 was their first launch at the new location on 25 September, when it landed in a stubble field at Castle Farm in Hoxne, some 20 miles from Ipswich.[2] There was minor damage to 12 houses.

Kenneth Boynes[3] in his diary

The only V2 specifically aimed at Ipswich exploded around 20 miles away in a field in Hoxne on 25 September 1944.

A Bomb No & time of fall	B Size & type of bomb & X or UX	C Judged by F, C or D	D Crater size and type of soil	E Location and damage notes ————— (Grid reference if no plot is made)	F Additional notes by R. & E. Dept. Technical Officers
				Map ref: 77/636936	
				HOXNE.	
I 1904	ROCKET projec- tile X.	F	30' x 12' Clay soil	In stubble field at Castle Farm. Slight damage to 12 houses. Furthest damage 1 mile from crater, nearest damage 500 yards. Slight swishing noise heard when object fell. Markings on large piece of aluminium – "Kr.202/bwo 3558" On small metal boxes 5" x 3" x 2" – "G R.K.11."; On piece of crepe paper – "01479".	
				Copy of East Suffolk Police Report. 27.9.44.	

Top of form:

SECRET   M. of H.S., R. & E. Dept. and AIR MINISTRY   BOMB CENSUS   FORM B.C.4.   COPY   Serial No.........   Sheet No. 1 ....

Region 4	County: E. Suffolk.		Total Casualties:	NIL	Date: 25/26.9.44
Adminis-trative Area	Hartismere R.D.		Killed M F C S/I M F C L/I M F C		Warnings P......... and R.....No....... Times W.warning......

The Ministry of Home Security, Research and Experiments Department made this report on the Hoxne V2 incident, based on the local police report.

noted, 'At about 7.10 pm on Monday September 25 a terrific explosion shook Ipswich. Current reports in the town later suggested that it was caused by one of the new rocket projectiles which came down near Diss.' Hoxne is around 3½ miles from Diss.

A young boy had been holding a large horse steady on a road near the outskirts of the village, when he saw the V2 drop vertically "looking like a dark line or a telegraph pole". He vividly remembered the flash and the amount of earth thrown into the air. The horse he had been holding bolted and he was pulled over. After initial concerns for the horse, he instinctively scrambled for cover as increasingly large clods of earth and stones began to rain down on him.

Appendices III and IV list the V2 incidents in Norfolk and Suffolk, while Figures 12.1 and 12.2 show their location. The compiler of the base log at Parham for 25 September noted 'Investigation of explosion heard earlier in the evening shows that it may have been V2 or buzz-bomb. Damn funny—all they found was a hole in the ground. No warning was given. Hell of a Blast!! (My mother writes to stay away from London).'

The V2 generally impacted at a steep angle and penetrated into the ground such that the explosion created a large crater; one at Ramsholt measured 50–60 feet.[4] To an extent this contained some of the blast effect. The V1 by contrast often produced a smaller crater but caused more blast damage as the explosion was near the surface.

The next Suffolk V2 fell at Hopton near Lowestoft on 3 October, but it had been aimed at Norwich. The local police sergeant was keen to make a full report, noting that no alert was given.[5]

> Numerous pieces of the projectile were found over an area approximately ¾ mile square, mostly to the E. of the crater. These pieces included three-quarter gear wheels attached to driving shafts, the wheels are similar to pedal cycle gear wheels, but somewhat heavier and with a triangular section missing; length of chain, similar to a motorcycle driving chain; large quantity of glass wool; much insulated wire and other electrical devices; metal cylinders; number of small wooden blocks; each 4 x 1½ x ¾ inch; and a quantity of 1 inch mesh wire netting; numerous pieces of copper and aluminium, some of which were covered with an oily liquid having a smell similar to that of methylated spirits. Also nearer to the crater were found a number of metal cylinders 2 ft long x 5 inch diameter; blocks of graphite; parts of a turbine motor and fuel tank.

The mighty V2 was thus consigned to a motley collection of mangled parts that would not have looked out of place in any scrap yard. The population at large had no real knowledge of the rocket threat and was not told that attacks had occurred until 10 November when Churchill made an announcement.

Norfolk residents were understandably concerned when random large explosions started to occur. The target for Batterie 444 was now Norwich with 43 V2s launched at the city, but the accuracy was fortunately very poor and many never made it to our shores. Some blew up on or near the launch pad, while others impacted in the sea or unknown locations. The Suffolk incidents on 3, 5 and 11 October were also the result of V2s aimed at Norwich. Between 26 September and 12 October, there were 27 incidents in Norfolk when V2s had been aimed at Norwich. Notes relating to some of these follow, along with first-hand recollections that were recorded by Steve Snelling.

26 September, Ranworth.[6] There was confusion when Norfolk's first V2 landed at 16.30. No one heard it approaching and the first sound heard was that of the double explosion. Norfolk's Civil Defence War Diary recorded the unfolding situation. First thoughts were that a high-explosive bomb had been dropped from an Allied plane. Then German markings were found on fragments, prompting further investigation. By the evening the general impression was that a plane had crashed. Then following further reports, Region (Regional Civil Defence HQ at Cambridge) at 22.45 stated that "previous information had substantially confirmed the type

of weapon suspected..." The next day there were three more such explosions heightening concerns over their origin. Then at 16.25, Region rang to enquire if they had any more information re suspected BIG BEN. As no one officially knew anything about the V2, the frustrated reply was "NO we are completely without guidance to enable us to detect what is or is not a BIG BEN."[7]

The peace of Rockland St Mary School was shattered on 4 October 1944 when a V2 exploded nearby. Flying faster than the speed of sound, there would be no audible warning of its approach.

3 October, Hellesdon. The impact was to the north of Norwich Golf Club and caused damage to 400 houses. Bert Homes, who lived closest to the impact, recalled "being blown across the room" as all the windows were shattered and the ceilings collapsed. It was incredible that no one was injured.

The Rockland St Mary incident report refers to nine casualties. Apart from the main crater, a second one was made by the venturi (outlet from combustion chamber).

4 October, Rockland St Mary. Ken Wilson was struck by flying debris and was one of 21 children who were hurt in this incident when a V2 exploded near his school. He recalled, "I hadn't got a clue what had happened. All I remember is the glass cutting at you like shale and being led out by a teacher." There was pandemonium as screaming children ran from the blizzards of flying glass. Other properties were extensively damaged but only one person was seriously injured. The incident was logged as a 'Bigben'.

4 October, Crostwick. Tommy Dungar had been watching a Liberator land at the nearby USAAF airfield at Rackheath. As he cycled away, for a fraction of a second he saw a "purple greyish shape, like a huge dart... followed by a terrible explosion." He then heard the second explosion. "The next thing I knew I was in the drainage ditch with [my] bicycle on top of me." Len Wilkinson along with his mother and sister were blown backwards through the doorway of their house, together with their furniture, fallen ceilings and broken glass. It felt as if the air had been sucked out of the room and it was several seconds before they could breathe again. A civilian worker at Rackheath Aero Club was thrown from her bicycle and suffered severe leg injuries from which she never fully recovered.

6 October, Shotesham. The teacher was reading *The Wind in the Willows* to the class when the explosion occurred at 09.25. Joy Leighton remembered that "all of a sudden there was an almighty crash and we all dived under our desks." Six-year-old John Anderson recalled that many were showered with broken glass and others cowered in the corners of the classroom. There was damage to property and large sections of debris from the rocket were strewn across the fields.

10 October, Bramerton. John and Denis Humphrey were blown 12 feet across their back yard. John recalled "It was one hell of an explosion. It just picked us up and threw us through the air." Their landlady's daughter was less fortunate as she was walking past their house and caught the full blast. "People said she came staggering back with virtually no clothes on and covered in a muddy soot-like substance."[8]

11 October, Rockland St Mary. It is difficult to believe, but a second V2 struck the village less than a mile from the first one. It impacted in a sugar beet field causing damage to about 15 houses and a glasshouse, but no casualties.

There would be two more Norfolk incidents, one on 26 October and the last on 7 March 1945, but those had strayed off their intended course to London. Memories of that time were also recalled by Joan Banger.[9]

At 6.10 on 26 September a very loud explosion was heard which seemed to come from the direction of Ranworth but no information could be obtained as to its origin. Then at 10.55 am the next day another explosion occurred north of the City and later on two more were heard, one from the general direction of Great Yarmouth and the other from the Bramerton area. At no time was any sign of a missile seen or heard. On 29 September there was an explosion at Coltishall followed by one at Whitlingham.

On 3 October 1944 at 7.45 pm the whole City was shaken by a large detonation and superficial blast damage to property in the Mile Cross and Dereham Road areas was reported. On the north side of Hellesdon Golf Course debris from a missile was strewn over an area of some 600 yards and a shallow crater 4 feet deep and 32 by 27 feet wide supplemented the bunkers on the course.

An ARP report referred to this missile as 'Big ben', their code word for the V2 rocket, which indeed it was. This terrible weapon that rained down on London that year was falling around our City but again fate decreed that none should fall within its boundaries.

In Suffolk, Boynes noted on 8 October: 'Recently rumours have been circulating in Ipswich, to the effect that rocket projectiles have been falling at various places in this country including London, Sheffield, Norwich, Yarmouth and Diss.' He did not have to wait long for one nearer home, as his diary entry for 11 October records, 'A tremendous explosion shook Wickham Market, Ipswich and Somersham. It was believed to be either an ammunition dump or a minefield being exploded…it is now known that it was a rocket projectile which came down between Rushmere and Playford causing a 30 foot crater and widespread superficial damage from blast.' This V2 was aimed at Norwich!

For 24 October, another diary entry records, 'The greatest explosion Ipswich has yet heard shook the town for nearly a minute. Reports suggested that it was caused by a V2 rocket projectile which came down in a field opposite Rushmere church.'

There had still been no official statement to acknowledge that the new form of vengeance weapon had already been unleashed against this country. Those affected by them already knew only too well. The rumour circulating was that these were gas-main explosions but nobody really believed that. A Mass Observation diarist in Bury St Edmunds referred to her friend, "Joyce says the Govt are so far hiding the fact that rockets are being sent over, and in one case where a certain well-known factory was damaged they put it down to an explosion at the gas-works."[10]

The last V2 fired from Rijsterbos towards Norfolk was on 12 October, which impacted at Manor Farm, Ingworth. The attention of the launch crews was then diverted to Antwerp, a very important port for the Allied forces. From 21 October Batterie 444 and 485 had moved to various sites in The Hague and were able to concentrate on their main target of London.

There were a total of 29 V2 incidents in Norfolk and 13 in Suffolk between 25 September and 7 March 1945. A further ten fell into the sea off the coast of Norfolk and Suffolk, again showing the inaccuracy and unreliability of such weapons, at the dawn of their development. The rural nature of the two counties meant that many of these missiles fell on open ground.

Lew Funk stands next to the combustion chamber of the V2 (now in N&S Aviation Museum) that exploded overhead near Stowupland on 20 February 1945.

The devastation when they landed in cities caused much loss of life. Extreme examples are the incident on 25 November when a V2 impacted on the Woolworths store in New Cross, London, killing 168 and injuring another 123. This was the highest loss of life in this country due to a V2 strike. In Antwerp on 16 December, the Rex cinema was packed with many soldiers, 567 people died in that terrible incident. On 8 March, 110 people were killed and 123 injured when a V2 struck Smithfield meat market. This was the final month for both V1 and V2 attacks in this country, but the devastation they caused was undiminished.

Boynes noted on 12 January, 'A terrific explosion shook the town as a V rocket fell near Trimley station. The concussion lasted several seconds.' There were five Suffolk V2 incidents in the first three months of 1945, which were mainly airbursts. These occurred at various times of the day and night, showering the area with high-temperature debris of both

A police sergeant views the crater made by the V2 that exploded near the bomb dump at USAAF Rackheath on 4 October 1944.

small and very large scale. Those living in the area of Old Newton and Gipping near Stowmarket were shaken from their beds by an overhead explosion of a V2 half an hour after midnight on 8 February. Debris rained down over an area 2½ miles long by half-a-mile wide. Only 12 days later the inhabitants of this area were

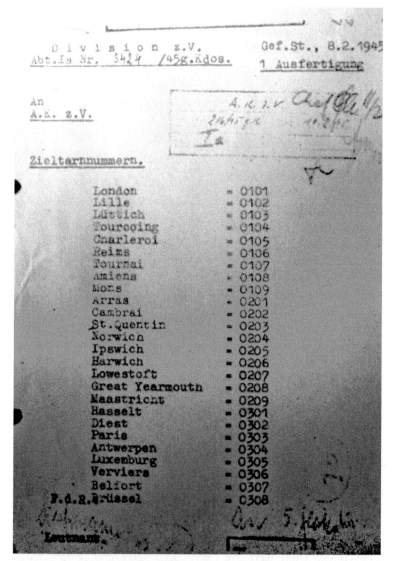

A German list of V2 targets from February 1945 included Harwich, Ipswich, Great
Yarmouth, Lowestoft and Norwich.

subjected to yet another airburst, this time near Stowupland some two miles away.

The ability to progress the V2 campaign was severely impeded by the relentless
Allied strikes on the launch-site areas and the associated infrastructure to supply
them. A German document dated 8 February 1945 sets out intended targets for
the V2. These were located in France, Belgium, and Luxembourg, plus of course
London. Other targets in England were Norwich, Ipswich, Harwich, Lowestoft and
Great Yarmouth. Their efforts against the first two were unsuccessful, but had the
war not been in its final stages, the implications for these other towns could have

been dire.

The last V2 to approach our area fell in the sea off Great Yarmouth on 22 March 1945, while the last against London was on 27 March, by which time the Allies had overrun the launch sites. A total of 1,359 V2s had been launched against London, of which 12 per cent failed shortly after launch, 10 per cent disintegrated in their final approach and nearly 78 per cent reached England. Civilians casualties were 2,754 killed and 6,523 seriously injured.[11]

Those living near the launch sites in Holland were at particular risk due to malfunctioning rockets. After one ascent the missile was seen to turn through 160 degrees and explode on housing, killing 38 residents. Those firing the missiles were also in danger. One V2 left the launch site and rose to about 100 yards before falling back onto the pad. The explosion killed 12 German soldiers and caused much damage to vehicles and equipment. Similar incidents were common.

The local population was also at great risk from air raids carried out on the suspected sites. The V2s were fired from mobile launchers located in areas where there was natural camouflage. There were many sites in The Hague and once launched, the team with all its vehicles would move into a wooded area making aerial identification extremely difficult.

A woman from Sudbury in Suffolk, Kathleen Hockley had married Peter Stein, a Dutchman, in 1936 and they went to live at The Hague. There was a V2 launch site near their home and she described the terrible experience when they were fired.[12] "There was a loud noise like thunder and a great sheet of flame. Very often the rockets came down again killing a lot of Dutch people and sometimes the Germans who launched them." Kathleen also recalled the harrowing conditions under which they all lived.

> The SS men were dreadful. We daren't open our mouths or they would shoot as soon as look at you. There were some nasty incidents such as a German soldier being found dead outside a row of house such as this. The Germans took ten men from those houses and simply shot them.

> The Germans took everything away—wireless, cycles and dogs. And we had orders to deliver up coats and blankets and silver articles…we had no lights, no gas, and we couldn't buy candles, and when it was dark we had to go to bed. If it was moonlight we could sit up.

> The food situation became very bad. We lived on sugar beet. My husband had a garden and so we had some potatoes and other vegetables, but some people had to eat tulip bulbs. As to bread, we had one very small loaf per head per week. There was some skim milk powder for children, but only infants under a year were allowed real milk. People used to walk miles into the country to get some greenstuff to eat.

This time last year Mr Stein, with other men, took to hiding under floor boards of houses in order to escape the continual search of the Germans for men for slave labour. He was hiding under one floor, off and on, for five days, only emerging when the 'coast was clear'. The Germans eventually got wise to this method of hiding and they used to go into the houses and shoot into the floor boards. If the housewife screamed or portrayed any anxiety the game was up. Mr Stein cut into the boards of his own bedroom so that if the Germans made a surprise visit at night he could immediately conceal himself…having got their quota of 'slave' Dutchmen they would go away for a time and then the dodging game was resumed during the quest for a fresh batch.

When the time of liberation was drawing near, the Dutch people hung out their flags, but the Germans shot at them and they had to take them in again…when British and American planes came over and began to drop food, the Dutch people ran into the streets laughing and crying. They then had no food at all. We could see the pilots in the planes and they dropped little packets they had brought themselves for children in the streets.

Between September 1944 and March 1945, there were the following number of V2 incidents in Norfolk and Suffolk.

	Sept.	Oct.	Nov.	Dec.	Jan.	Feb.	March
Norfolk	8	20	0	0	0	0	1
Suffolk	1	4	1	2	2	3	0

Batterie 444 was responsible for most of the incidents that occurred in Norfolk and Suffolk up until the end of 1944. For the final three months of the campaign in 1945, the missiles were fired mainly from Batterie 485. There were no fatalities from V2s in Norfolk or Suffolk, but many people were injured and many buildings damaged. Had these weapons been developed earlier, the outcome might have been very different.

The following websites provide a wealth of information on V2 incidents and the compilers are thanked for their extensive research and the information provided.

http://www.v2rocket.com and http://www.wrsonline.co.uk

Notes

1. Mick Muttitt, 2 September 2022.
2. The National Archives (TNA), HO 198/103, Bomb Census Reports, Long Range Rockets, Region 4.
3. Suffolk Archives (SA), HD 3071, Diary of K. W. Boynes.
4. Ibid., 2
5. SA, A 1608/1, Daily Situation Reports 1944.
6. Ibid., 2.

7. Norfolk Record Office (NRO), C/ARP2/5, Civil Defence War Diary.

8. *Britain at War*, Key Publishing, September 2018.

9. Banger, J., *Norwich at War*, Poppyland Publishing, 2003, pp. 89–90.

10. Mass Observation Diary, Ref. 5271.

11. O'Brien, T. H., History of the Second World War; Civil Defence, HMSO and Longmans, Green, 1955, Appendices II and V.

12. *Suffolk and Essex Free Press*, 22 November 1945.

Epilogue

The Armistice was signed on 7 May 1945, ending the Second World War in Europe. For those on the Home Front it was a great relief. Many had lost friends and family in the conflict, and life would never be quite the same again. The bombing raids on the UK in the earlier part of the war were pre-empted by the wailing of the sirens. Pause to think for a moment. You are woken by the siren in the middle of a winter's night. Your options are to ignore it and risk your life or grab some clothes and rush to the Anderson shelter in the garden. You might then endure a long wait on a bench in freezing conditions before the all-clear sounded. The indoor Morrison table-shelter, introduced in 1941, was much preferred to other forms of shelter that were available.

Many small towns and villages did not have the luxury of an air-raid warning siren. They had to rely on wardens running through the streets blowing whistles and knocking on doors. Framlingham is a case in point. After suffering two raids where lives were lost, their application for a siren was turned down as the population did not meet the minimum size criterion. Residents of the town then clubbed together and bought their own. Later in the war, the number of conventional raids had considerably reduced, but the onset of the V1 offensive meant the sound of the dreaded siren would continue to cause anxiety. When a V1 was heard, everyone willed it to keep going.

Ipswich had been subject to many raids in the early war years. By late 1944 the tide of the war was turning, with the Home Guard being stood down and various defences being dismantled. This was the very time when the V1s were most active over the town, and the sirens continued to provide the necessary warning. The Anderson shelter was effective as protection from blast damage at a distance, but nothing could withstand a direct hit such as occurred at Halton Crescent on 18 October. Boynes noted that the Ipswich sirens had sounded 1,163 times throughout the war.

In coastal areas, the barrage put up by the AA guns created noise and deadly shrapnel. There was the knowledge that the guns were trying to bring down V1s which, if hit, could explode near or even on you. By the end of March it was all over. The 63 AA Brigade War Diary noted on 24 April: 'Diver activity considered to have ceased, therefore The Diver Gun Strip and all rules pertaining thereto are suspended.' When visiting Thorpeness or any coastal location, spare a thought for those who had to contend with all that.

The V-weapon campaign has been the subject of much discussion ever since. Such matters are complex and generally beyond the scope of this book. However, a few points to consider.

Hitler had little interest in V-weapons in the early part of the war as he was confident of victory using conventional warfare methods. It was not until later when the Allied raids on German cities intensified that they were seen by him as a way to strike directly at England. The decision to provide all the funding was taken too late and by the time of the first V1 launches in June 1944, those sites were already being overrun by the Allies. Had they taken place a year or more earlier, the outcome might have been different. Alternatively, had those costs been spent on more tanks and aircraft rather than V-weapons, this may also have altered the balance of the war.

The V1 was a relatively simple and cost-effective weapon, whereas the V2 was much larger and contained much sophisticated technology which would all be destroyed in the impact. The one thing they had in common was that they both delivered a similar weight of explosive. The V2 therefore, did not make economic sense at the time in terms of payload delivered. So, why was it progressed at such an enormous financial and human cost? Professor R. V. Jones was Assistant Director of Intelligence at the Air Ministry during the war. In his book *Most Secret War*, he said 'I suspected that Hitler had been carried away by the romance of the rocket, just as our own politicians had been carried away by the threat: for some psychological reason they seemed far more frightened by one ton of explosive delivered by rocket than by five tons delivered by aircraft.'

From the Allies point of view, massive resources were eventually employed to combat the V-weapon threat. A heavy human price was paid in terms of all the bomber crews who were lost while delivering vast quantities of ordnance onto the sites. In the UK there were over 60,000 civilians killed by all forms of enemy action in the war and of that number nearly 15 per cent were due to V-weapons. There was also a huge economic cost when all the aircraft, bombs, barrage balloons, AA guns, damage to factories, loss of production, repairs to houses and many other factors were taken into account.

The Allies all saw the potential in the V-weapons and there was an undignified scramble to secure the top German scientists to lead their own developments in the post-war period. Wernher von Braun and many other leading scientists were hastily taken to the United States where they went on to develop rockets to explore outer space and land the first man on the moon. It should not be forgotten that von Braun was a member of the Nazi party and made visits to the slave-labour camps, so knew the horrendous conditions there only too well. The great achievements of the space race have a dark history.

Notes to Appendices I to IV

The V1 and V2 incidents in Norfolk and Suffolk are listed in Appendices I to IV. The information has been obtained from a number of sources. The National Archives AIR 20 series listed below provide a date, time and place name for each incident. If they were outside London they came under a heading 'Elsewhere', for which map references are provided. These are essential as several well known names such as Parham, Easton and Henham are listed, but they are not always the ones we know in Suffolk, but in other parts of the country.

For specific information on individual incidents, the following sources have been consulted:

THE NATIONAL ARCHIVES (TNA),

HO198/77, 78. Eastern Region Flying Bomb Reports.

HO198/170, 171, 172. Flying Bomb summaries 12 June to 24 December.

AIR20/3684, 3685. Summary of Flying Bomb attacks 1June to March 1945.

AIR 20/4128, 4129. List of Flying Bomb Incidents 1July to March 1945.

WO166/14537, 54 Division War Diaries, East Suffolk.

NORFOLK RECORD OFFICE (NRO)

C/ARP 1/33. Incident sheets, June 1943 to April 1945.

C/ARP 2/49-58. Norfolk County Council Civil Defence War Diaries.

SUFFOLK ARCHIVES (SA)

A1608/1, 3. Suffolk Constabulary reports and Enemy Bombs in East Suffolk.

A1609/2. Fortnightly Situation Reports.

DC/2, 3, 4. Ipswich Borough Air Raid Reports.

HD 862/3. Ipswich Raid Reports.

The original map references have been used to provide a location name that is nearest to the incident. In rural areas the location may be some distance from any town or village. Individual reports for such incidents often show variations in the named location, map reference, number and degree of damage to buildings and also the injuries sustained. The cumulative data from these sources have been evaluated to provide the description in the appendices. The county location pertains to the period and not any more recent boundary changes. Hopton near Lowestoft was in Suffolk then, but is now in Norfolk. The original names of houses and farms etc. in the incident reports have been used, which may have since changed.

The original maps were known as the Cassini Ordnance Survey Second War Revision and are based on a one kilometre square. Each reference was given three figures for each Easting and Northing. This in turn defines an area which is 100 metres square. The site of the incident could be anywhere in that area, so precise location is not usually possible unless there is additional recorded detail such as buildings names etc. The Cassini references have been converted to modern Ordnance Survey (OS) coordinates. By selecting the map for the area of the incident, the coordinates in the appendices allow the approximate location of the incident to be determined.

There is often more detail in the original reports than can be shown in the appendices. In some cases though, there is no supporting information in which case a blank is shown. This likely suggests that it exploded on farm land causing no damage. The effects of bomb damage to property were generally categorised as follows:

Category A (Cat-A). Totally destroyed.

Category B (Cat-B). Badly damaged and demolition necessary.

Category C   (Cat-C). Seriously damaged but capable of repair.

Category D (Cat-D). Minor damage.

Suffolk reports did not always use the category ratings, but gave a description on the above lines. Norfolk regularly used the rating system. The most common rating is Category D for minor damage. This could mean a broken window or dislodged tiles which accounts for some incidents where hundreds of properties were damaged.

Appendix I

AA = Hit by Anti-Aircraft gunfire. ALD = Air-Launched Doodlebug

Map No.	Date	OS Map Ref.	Time and Location	Additional Information
1	10 July	TF935030	02.17. Ovington, College Farm	No casualties. Minor damage. First ALD
2	31 July	TG002086	03.40. Whinburgh, Manor House. Seen over Felixstowe 03.31 heading NNW	Extensive damage to MH, slight damage to school, church and cottages. 8 slight injuries. Evacuees re-billeted. Ramp launch
3	24 Sept.	TG212001	04.41. Swainsthorpe, in field 200yds N of Brick Kiln Yard	Rail line blocked. Trees felled. Cat-D 5 houses. AA. Map Nos. 3-13 all ALD
4	9 Oct.	TM336954	05.05. Thwaite St Mary, hit tree in meadow at Hall Farm, 300 yds from Bungay Road	Slight damage to farmhouse, church and 8 houses
5	13 Oct.	TF889135	21.32. Great Fransham. Field House Farm S of railway station	Exploded in air. Cat-D to farmhouse, 12 houses in Fransham, 6 in Beeston and 6 in Great Dunham.
6	13 Oct.	TF865978	21.45. Cressingham, battle training area, 300 yds SE of Arms Crossroads	Cat-C 3 houses, Cat-D 17 houses. 4 slightly injured.
7	19 Oct.	TM424987	05.15. Thurlton, White House Farm, on marshland	Cat-D 12 houses. AA

8	4 Nov.	TL950946	19.20. Breckles, Grange Farm, in field	Cat-D to Breckles Hall and church
9	10 Nov.	TG129012	19.45. Wymondham, in field at Banhams Farm	Cat-D to Browick Hall, Banhams Farm and 6 houses. 1 person slightly injured
10	18 Dec.	TG823971	06.03. Langford, glided down onto battle training area	V1 cut out over Kimberley. Cat-D to Bodney Hall and plantation.
1945				
11	3 Jan.	TM029999	18.57. Deopham Green on USAAF airfield	Detonation near corner of base. Cat-D 5 cottages
12	3 Jan.	TG391226	19.43. Between Sutton and Catfield, in lane at Neave's Farm	Fell as UXB. 11 people evacuated. Blown up by Bomb Disposal in situ on 14 Jan. AA
13	3 Jan.	TM262926	20.00. Topcroft, in field at Rookery Farm	Cat-D 20 houses. USAAF removed remains. AA

Appendix II

SUFFOLK

LOCATION OF V1 INCIDENTS ON LAND

1944 AND 1945

AA=Hit by Anti-Aircraft gunfire. ALD=Air Launched Doodlebug
The direction from which the V1 came is noted when known, e.g. From S

Map No.	Date	OS Map Ref.	Time and Location	Additional Information
1	16 June	TM340700	00.28. Peasenhall, in field at Lodge Farm	Airburst. Blast damage to houses. Remains in N&S Aviation Museum

2	16 June	TM175379	16.13. Woolverstone, in field off Harkstead Lane	Slight damage to houses, ceilings down
3	26 June	TM315673	15.20. Badingham, in beet field near Coulston Hall	Damage to Coulston Hall buildings, Mill House, Old Rectory
4	28 June	TM306431	22.40. Shottisham, on marshes	Damage to Sutton Hall, Laundry Villas, Wood Hall
5	2 July	TL749460	14.15. Clare, Leys Farm, in field next to Maple Road	1½ acres wheat burnt out
6	7 July	TM229679	13.01. Worlingworth, in field at Poplar Farm. From SE	Minor damage to 8 properties. Disruption to school
7	13 July	TM259363	10.15. Trimley St Martin, in field at Grimston Hall Farm. From S	No damage
8	18 July	TM079622	22.27. Gipping, in lane beside Gipping Wood near Woods Farm.	Struck tree and exploded before hitting ground. Damage to Wood Farm. First ALD in Suffolk
9	19 July	TM279663	11.59. Framlingham. In field 300 yds NE of Framlingham Hall near Dennington. From S	Damage to roofs and windows of Hall, Dairy Farm House and Hall Cottages. Blast damage to 2 acres wheat
10	25 July	TM439552	23.30. Iken. In battle area.	No damage
11	27 July	TL656461	01.33. Withersfield, in field near Haverhill	Shot down by plane. 1 person slightly injured. Damage to houses in Haverhill and Withersfield

12	28 July	TM372615	22.46. Benhall, near Walnut Tree Cottage. From S	Considerable damage to 3 houses, slight damage to 14
13	29 July	TL883473	01.37. Long Melford, near Bassett's Farm	
14	12 Aug.	TL976404	01.35. Boxford, near Tills Farm	
15	13 Aug.	TL908535	06.20. Cockfield, in field at Mill Farm	Severe blast damage to 25 houses
16	15 Aug.	TL734482	18.04. Hundon, Pinhoe Hall Farm, in ditch	Hall, farm and buildings badly damaged
17	18 Aug.	TM243484	07.24. Great Bealings, in meadow at Rosary Farm. From S/SSW	Powered dive into ground. 2 craters. Damage to farmhouse and 12 other houses. 1 injured
18	19 Aug.	TL766490	14.52. Poslingford	
19	23 Aug.	TL748526	09.19. Stradishall, in field next to Hound Inn	Damage to Church, vicarage, school, Post Office, Stradishall Place, Hound Inn and other houses
20	30 Aug.	TM405603	13.54. Friston, in field SE of the Hall. From SE	
21	31 Aug.	TM071404	04.50. Great Wenham, 300yds S of Vauxhall Farm. From E	Slight damage to farmhouse, buildings and crops. ALD
22	31 Aug.	TM084366	04.45. Capel St Mary, 300yds E of Chaplain's Farm cottages. From NE	Slight damage to Chaplain's Cottages, Highfields, Cotswold Poultry Farm, Sunny Bank cottages and garage. ALD

23	31 Aug.	TM058413	04.35. Raydon, SE of Kate's Hill Farm, in Tom's Wood. From E	Exploded in trees, no crater. Slight damage to Hadleigh Farm and cottages. Also houses in Hintlesham and Chattisham. ALD
24	31 Aug.	TM016613	04.45. Harleston, near Stowmarket. 100 yds E of Moorbridge Farm. From E	Cat-C 2 houses, Cat-D 2 houses. 7 people slightly injured. ALD
25	1 Sept.	TM189422	02.18. Ipswich. Fell in Maryon Road	4 bungalows demolished, 495 buildings damaged. 1 killed, 31 injured
26	1 Sept.	TM157387	02.20. Freston, Cutler's Wood. From E	4 houses slightly damaged
End of Phase 1 ramp-launched V1s				**All ALD in Phase 2**
27	5 Sept.	TM300374	05.08. Felixstowe, King's Fleet marshes. From E	Just missed Bawdsey CH transmitter towers. Exploded on marshes
28	20 Sept.	TL922542	01.40. Cockfield, Bulls Wood Lane, hit tree	Warhead separated and exploded. Body of V1 mainly complete. Damage to buildings
29	20 Sept.	TM349786	20.48. Chediston, 120 yds E of Grove Farm. From NE	Damage to Grove Cottage Farm and buildings. 4 stacks burnt down, machinery destroyed
30	21 Sept.	TM360412	04.27. Bawdsey, on beach. From NE	Explosion detonated 57 beach mines. AA
31	21 Sept.	TM316573	04.44. Hacheston, in field ¾ mile NE of Bridge Farm. From NE	Damage to 3 houses, 1 girl slightly injured
32	24 Sept.	TM213576	04.45. Framsden, 450yds E of Bastings Hall	Damage to Hall and 2 cottages

33	24 Sept.	TL926606	22.04. Hessett, in Mellfield Woods	Damage to Hill Farm, Freewood Farm and Mellfield Cottage
34	29 Sept.	TM188373	05.15. Woolverstone, in Bylam Wood. From NE	Light damage to 40 houses. AA
35	29 Sept.	TL774641	05.23. Barrow, Burthorpe Farm	Damage to farm
36	29 Sept.	TL934434	05.23. Edwardstone, near Lynn's Hall	
37	5 Oct.	TM140354	19.53. Stutton, 88 yds E of Holly Farm	Severe damage to farmhouse, slight damage to 5 houses. 1 person seriously injured, 1 slightly
38	5 Oct.	TM456509	19.54. Orford, on beach	Damage to 16 houses
39	8 Oct.	TL942376	20.00. Assington, Aveley Hall Farm	Airburst. Damage to Hall and church. AA
40	9 Oct.	TM463798	00.32. Wangford, in field near Elms Farm. Map ref. query, possibly 473798	19 houses damaged. Severe damage to Elms Farm. 2 stacks on fire. AA
41	9 Oct.	TM403643	00.55. Kelsale, hit tree 100 yds W of Clay Hills Farm	Severe damage to farmhouse and bungalow. Lesser damage to White House and Oak Tree farms plus several houses on perimeter of USAAF Leiston
42	9 Oct.	TL945399	00.35. Assington, in Vicarage Field. N of Aveley Hall	

43	12 Oct.	TM341607	23.55. Stratford St Andrew, in field at Grove Farm	Power dived to ground. Damage to 7 cottages. 250 yds from USAAF bomb dump at Parham. AA
44	12 Oct.	Approx. 3748	23.46. Capel St Andrew	Airburst
45	13 Oct.	TL816663	21.45. Westley, Hyde Wood, 100 yds from cottages	Cottages and farm buildings damaged
46	14 Oct.	TM519010	20.25. Hopton, near Gorleston. Close to High Cottages. Failed to explode. From E	The next day an RE officer was killed and 1 injured when fuse and detonator exploded. AA
47	14 Oct.	TL684736	03.28. Worlington, in meadow at Rectory Farm, 1 mile W of Mildenhall	Farmhouse evacuated and houses damaged. 1 slightly injured
48	14 Oct.	TM505762 through TM505772 to sea	20.00. Southwold. Airburst over town	About 300 houses, 57 shops, 9 business premises and 3 churches damaged. Estimates vary. 1 casualty. AA
49	14 Oct.	TM531930	20.14. Lowestoft. Glided into Lake Lothing and exploded. From NE	Damage to factories, railway, 255 properties and 2 schools. AA
50	15 Oct.	TL967344	02.08. Nayland, in Lewis meadow, Bear Street	Shot down by fighter plane. Many houses damaged, Police Station evacuated. Several people injured
51	16 Oct.	TM536878	04.54. Kessingland, on beach	20 houses damaged. Defence scaffolding on beach destroyed

52	16 Oct.	TM280373	04.58. Trimley St Mary, in stackyard at Limes Farm	30 houses, 4 other buildings and 2 churches damaged
53	16 Oct.	TM529838	05.12. Benacre, airburst over Beach Farm	Farmhouse, huts, tents and 20 houses in Kessingland damaged
54	18 Oct.	TM194424	23.27. Ipswich, 5 Halton Crescent. V1 hit Anderson shelter in rear garden	4 killed, 19 injured. 4 houses destroyed, 4 to be demolished. 33 to be evacuated, 11 useable. 340 plus slight damage. AA
55	19 Oct.	TM507929	05.12. Oulton Broad, in trees near Mancroft Towers. From E	Cat-B 1house, Cat-C 3, Cat-D 2. Further 150 slightly damaged. 2 injured. AA
56	19 Oct.	TL876496	05.25. Alpheton, in field at Tye Farm	Damage to property
57	19 Oct.	TM373479	20.15. Capel St Andrew, hit trees, 20 yds from Laurel Farm House	Severe damage to farmhouse. Damage to 5 houses, 1 injury. AA
58	20 Oct.	TM292456	05.00. Sutton, in River Deben	Superficial damage to 16 buildings in Sutton, Waldringfield and Woodbridge
59	21 Oct.	TM073521	04.50. Barking, Andrews Farm, close to Bonny Wood	Minor damage to farm and 48 houses in Barking, Ringshall and Wattisham
60	24 Oct.	TM402586	00.55. Snape. Hit tree and exploded in air over buildings at Rookery Farm	Farmhouse and buildings demolished, 18 houses damaged. 2 men seriously injured, 9 cattle killed. AA
61	25 Oct.	TM255444	19.30. Brightwell, in spinney on heath	Damage to Nos. 1 and 2 Heath Cottages. AA

62	29 Oct.	TM359451	05.10. Hollesley, in field 500 yds E of Duck Corner	Damage to Glebe House and about 15 other houses. Jet unit found in crater. AA
63	31 Oct.	Approx. TM4554	07.55. Sudbourne. Exploded in air over marshes. From NE	In battle area. No damage. AA
64	4 Nov.	TM250389	19.13. Stratton Hall, Levington, 30 yds from cottages	Sea Bridge Cottages badly damaged. Stratton House, farm and buildings damaged. 1 killed, 1 seriously injured. 3 children and 1 adult slightly injured
65	5 Nov.	TM460586	20.20. Aldeburgh, Gorse Hill. Hit AA site close to ROC post. House in Clouds hit by Bofors shell	Warhead did not explode. 5 military personnel suffered burns, 1 later died. Much equipment destroyed by fire. AA.
66	6 Nov.	TM402664	20.35. Kelsale, East Green, in trees at Rubblestone Farm	Minor damage to Rubblestone and Red House farms and 8 cottages. Remains are in N&S Aviation Museum. AA
67	6 Nov.	TM461686	20.18. Westleton, ½ mile E of Walk Barn Farm	No damage. AA
68	10 Nov.	TM283524	19.50. Ufford, near Grove Farm. Hit tree, exploded about 20 feet above ground	Damage to farm, St Audrey's hospital and Ufford Police Station. AA
69	10 Nov.	TM247340	19.58. Shotley, on grounds at HMS Ganges, ¼ mile NNE of Shotley Gate	Cat-C 2 houses, Cat-D 24 houses. Damage to HMS Ganges buildings. AA

70	11 Nov.	TM406519	01.33. Sudbourne estate. Fell in Watling Wood, about ½ mile N of Sudbourne Hall	Damage to Hall, 6 cottages and glasshouses. 2 injured. Children trapped but unhurt. AA
71	14 Nov.	TM300397	18.59. Falkenham, about 100 yds S of Lower Farm	Lower Farm cottages extensively damaged. 10 others slightly damaged. 1 serious injury. AA
72	14 Nov.	TM438677	18.50. Middleton, in marsh about 83 yds E of Lackford Bridge	Damage to Lackford Farm and 4 houses. AA
73	14 Nov.	TM346589	18.58. Little Glemham, in trees 200 yds S of Glemham Hall	Damage to Hall, church, rectory and 4 cottages. AA
74	14 Nov.	TM258461	19.14. Martlesham, in trees at edge of aerodrome	Damage to huts and 30 houses. 2 serious injuries and 2 slight. AA
75	19 Nov.	TM515901	19.57. Carlton Colville, in yard at Low Farm. Explosion occurred approximately 45 seconds after 'the light disappeared'. From E	Low Farm Cottages 2 Cat-A. Other houses Cat-C 6, Cat-D 110. Also, minor damage to 80 houses and church. 2 women killed, 17 injured. Propaganda leaflets found. Probably AA
76	23 Nov.	TM156394	00.55. Wherstead, burst on impact in trees. N edge of Cutler's Wood	6 houses damaged in Wherstead, 15 in Freston including church. AA
77	23 Nov.	TM424537	01.12. Sudbourne, in battle training area 30 yds E of Captain's Wood. From E	No damage. AA

78	24 Nov.	TL982413	06.10. Polstead, Bower House	Tubes contained leaflets 'The Other Side of Berlin No. 2'
79	10 Dec.	TM206373	18.50. Chelmondiston, direct hit on Myrtle Cottage, close to church	Cat-A Myrtle Cottage, Cat-B 3, Cat-C, 19, Cat-D 60 properties. Church almost destroyed. 1 killed, 4 serious injuries, 17 slightly injured. AA
80	10 Dec.	TM239397	18.53. Levington, in trees 400 yds NE of Red House Farm	Damage to Red House, White House and Bridge Farms, Levington Hall and greenhouses at Nacton House. Propaganda leaflets found. AA
81	11 Dec.	TM531987	22.40. Hopton. In field at Woburn Farm. From NE	Did not explode, broke up on impact. Large sections of wreckage scattered. AA
82	12 Dec.	TM287754	19.49. Fressingfield, in field ESE of Rookery Farm.	Damage to farm and Elm Lodge, 3 houses and bungalow. AA
83	18 Dec.	TM268359	03.54. Trimley St Martin, in Painters Wood near Grimston Hall Farm. From NE	Damage to Grimston Hall, Alston Hall and 4 other properties. AA
84	18 Dec.	TM327452	04.30. Shottisham, in field at Vale Farm	Damage to Broxstead House and Brook House. AA
85	18 Dec.	TM194382	04.48. Woolverstone, in field at White House Farm. About ½ mile S of Woolverstone Hall	Cat-D 12 properties including the school and Woolverstone Hall. AA

86	18 Dec.	TM222623	04.00. Cretingham, in field 200 yds from Stone House Farm, ½ mile NW of Cretingham Lodge	Damage to Ashfield Farm buildings, church, Cretingham Lodge, High Row and Hill farms. AA
87	18 Dec.	TM411478	03.59. Gedgrave marshes, Orford. About ½ mile SE of Gedgrave Hall. From E	No damage. Hit by AA fire, small explosion followed by another, then dived into marshes
1945				
88	3 Jan.	TM523991	19.50. Hopton, in field at Elm Farm, 250 yds S of Jay Lane	Damage to 12 houses. AA
89	3 Jan.	TM449571	18.35. Aldeburgh, in field about ¼ mile W of Aldeburgh Hall. From NE	Crossed coast on fire, cleared town centre. Cat-C damage to Iken Way house and less to 13 others. AA
90	3 Jan.	TM440867	19.16. Ellough, in field about ¼ mile WSW of church	Clipped church flagpole. Damage to church and 13 houses. AA
91	3 Jan.	TM268513	19.01. Bredfield, in trees about ¼ mile SE of Bredfield House	Lodge demolished. Damage to 3 houses. 2 seriously injured. AA
92	13 Jan.	TM367492	06.05. Capel St Andrew, in mud at Green Farm	Did not explode. Extricated with great difficulty. AA
End of Phase 2. Last ALD on 14 January				**Phase 3 begins with renewed ramp launches only on 3 March**
93	19 March	TM108727	09.16. Thornham Parva, in field at Chandos Farm	Slight damage to farmhouse. Warhead also contained incendiaries

Appendix III

NORFOLK

LOCATION OF V2 INCIDENTS ON LAND

1944 AND 1945

MAP NOS. 1 TO 27–TARGET NORWICH

All crater dimensions in feet

Map No.	Date	OS Map Ref	Time and Location	Additional Information
1	26 Sept.	TG349150	16.30. Ranworth, in field	Crater 25 deep. Damage to church, vicarage and Malsters Inn. 1 slight injury
2	27 Sept.	TG192187	10.48. Botany Bay Farm, in trees. N of Horsford	Crater 40 by 11. Minor damage
3	27 Sept.	TG895074	16.25. Exploded over Horning Ferry. Impact at Whitlingham close to sewage works, N of Kirby Bedon	Cat-D to Whitlingham Farm, 5 houses, store sheds and greenhouse. Pea stacks destroyed. 2 injured
4	27 Sept.	TG386095	17.50. Exploded over Stokesby. Impact in field at Acle Hall Farm N of Beighton, 50 yds from rail line	Cat-D to farm, houses at Beighton and Acle. Damage to railway tracks and to telegraph wires
5	29 Sept.	TG508178	13.11. Hemsby, in minefield on beach. Area occupied by military	Crater 40 dia. Cat-D to 6 houses, 2 shops and 60 bungalows
6	29 Sept.	TG277195	19.44. Coltishall, in marshland near Manor House	Crater 40 dia. Cat-D to 27 houses. 3 men slightly injured, livestock killed

7	29 Sept.	TG260078	20.41. Between Thorpe St Andrew and Whitlingham, in sugar beet field	Crater 31x12. Cat-D to 25 houses and Post Office
8	30 Sept.	TG411085	12.14. Tunstall, near Acle, in open country W of Staithe Farm	Crater 30 x 15. Cat-D to 8 houses, farmhouse and barn
9	1 Oct.	TM278909	17.55. Bedingham, in field at Sycamore Farm, close to USAAF Hardwick hospital	Crater 30 x 15. Cat-C to farm buildings. Cat-D to 5 houses. 4 injured
10	3 Oct.	TG329218	09.30. Beeston St Lawrence, in field about 400 yds E of church, 700 yds from Beeston Hall	Crater 33 x 9. Cat-D to church, Beeston Hall, 5 houses and Irstead church
11	3 Oct.	TG095210	16.55. Great Witchingham, in field at Mill Farm	Crater 54 dia. Cat-D to 6 properties with windows broken, ceilings down. 1 injured
12	3 Oct.	TG207115	19.50. Hellesdon. Disintegrated over Mile Cross housing estate. Warhead hit Royal Norwich Golf Club	Explosion in air and on ground. Crater 33 x 37 x 12 deep. Cat-D to 298 houses. 1 slight injury
13	3 Oct.	TM257893	20.00. Denton, in field at Darrow Farm	Crater 46 x 33 x 12 deep. Cat-D to farmhouse and outbuildings
14	4 Oct.	TG314038	13.41. Rockland St Mary, about 200 yds from school	Crater 24 x 12. Cat-C to house, rectory and Star Inn. Cat-D to 25 houses. Serious injury to 1 man, light injuries to 8 or more children and 1 teacher

15	4 Oct.	TG266164	16.48. Crostwick, Mud Corner. About ¼ mile from bomb dump at USAAF Rackheath	Crater 44 x 34. Cat-D to Old Hall Farm, buildings and 2 cottages. 1 serious injury
16	4 Oct.	TG244143	17.37. Spixworth, disintegrated in air, debris scattered over large area	Cat-D to 4 houses and church. Major parts of rocket sent to Research Institute at Farnborough
17	5 Oct.	TG148130	09.04. Taverham. In wood at Taverham Hall Farm	Crater 43 x 33 x 10 deep. Severe damage to trees
18	5 Oct.	TG320063	13.28. Surlingham, disintegrated in air, debris scattered over fields	Cat-C to 6 houses. Cat-D to 30 houses and church. 10 slightly injured
19	5 Oct.	TM421097	16.10. Tunstall, ESE of Acle, in dyke beside A12	Crater 54 x 50 x 5 deep. Road blocked. Cat-D to 3 houses.
20	5 Oct.	TG303127	17.44. Little Plumstead, exploded in mid air. Crater in field at Heath Farm	Crater 36 x 12. Cat-D to farmhouse at 300yds. Metal scattered over large area
21	6 Oct.	TM246988	09.25. Shotesham All Saints, in woods SW of church	Crater 33 x 15. Cat-D to 20 houses, shop and rectory. 2 slight injuries
22	9 Oct.	TG385031	10.45. Cantley, in dyke 400yds from Sugar Beet factory	Crater 45 x 35 x 10. Cat-D to cottage and factory. 2 cattle killed
23	9 Oct.	TM301996	10.50. Brooke, in field at Hillside Farm, 300 yds from Brooke Hall	2 craters each 27 by 5. Cat-D to Hall, lodge and farm
24	10 Oct.	TG292058	17.55. Bramerton, in meadow at Woods End	Crater 42 x 11. Cat-D to farm buildings and 22 houses. 2 injured

25	11 Oct.	TM428966	08.10. Haddiscoe, in field about 500 yds from Hall	Crater 32 by 10. Cat-D to Haddiscoe Hall and 4 cottages
26	11 Oct.	TG316049	10.51. Rockland St Mary, in sugar beet field	Crater 50 x 15. Cat-D to about 15 houses and glasshouse
27	12 Oct.	TG189301	07.40. Ingworth, in field	Crater 31 x 11. Cat-D to 24 houses, church and farm buildings. Damage also in Erpingham
28	26 Oct.	TG061091	10.14. Welbourne, in field	Crater 41 x 13. Cat-D to farmhouse, school and 20 houses. 2 slight injuries
1945				
29	7 March	TM400950	14.50. Brundish, Cluttons Farm, south of Raveningham	Crater 40 dia. x 18 deep. Damage to electricity cables

Appendix IV

SUFFOLK

LOCATION OF V2 INCIDENTS ON LAND

1944 AND **1945**

All crater dimensions in feet

Map No.	Date	OS Map Ref.	Time and Location	Additional Information
1	25 Sept.	TM183755	19.04. Hoxne, in field at Castle Farm	Crater 30 x 12. Minor damage to 12 houses. Only V2 targeted on Ipswich

2	3 Oct.	TM530014	14.40. Hopton, near Gorleston, in field at Valley Farm, 100 yds W of railway line	Crater 18 x 5. Major damage to nearby buildings, minor up to 500yds. 3 serious injuries, 5 slight. Target Norwich
3	5 Oct.	TM360710	11.38. Peasenhall, in field ½ mile E of Manor Farm	Minor damage to houses about 400 yds away. Target Norwich
4	11 Oct.	TM212468	14.20. Playford, in field	Crater 39 x 13. Minor damage to barn, and houses up to 2 ½ miles. 2 straw stacks burnt out. Target Norwich
5	24 Oct.	TM198460	04.57. Rushmere St Andrew, in field about 500 yds SEE of church	Crater 36 x 8. Minor damage to about 70 houses up to ¾ mile
6	29 Nov.	TL772497	19.50. Poslingford, disintegrated in air	Crater 27 x 7. Slight damage to Flax Farm, Edmunds Farm and 6 cottages. Parts of V2 used by authorities to construct replica
7	2 Dec.	TM310408	07.35. Ramsholt, on mudflats about ½ mile W of Poplar Farm	Crater 55 dia. Minor damage to farmhouse, 700 yds from crater
8	23 Dec.	TL671745	23.46. West Row, nr Mildenhall. Airburst ½ mile from Jude's Ferry	Crater 44 x 8. Fragments fell over wide area
			1945	
9	5 Jan.	TM039400	09.25. Layham. Airburst	Fragments fell over wide area. Minor damage to dwellings over about ½ mile

10	12 Jan.	TM272367	17.37. Trimley St Mary. Airburst. Impact in field at Great Street Farm, about 17 yds S of railway line	Crater 45 x 8. Damage to railway track and several houses.
11	8 Feb.	TM081636 TM045641	00.32. Gipping near Old Newton. Airburst	Fragments found over area 2 ½ miles long by ½ mile wide
12	13 Feb.	TL781555	16.39. Depden, in field at Elms Farm	Light damage to property up to 600 yds
13	20 Feb.	TL097604 TL080608	09.55. NE of Stowupland. Airburst between Upland Farm and Gipping Farm	Fragments scattered over large area. Propulsion unit in N&S Aviation Museum

Appendix V

V-WEAPON INCIDENTS AND CASUALTIES

1944–1945

INCIDENTS	V1 +	V2 *
London (Region)	2,420	517
Kent	1,444	64
Sussex	886	4
Essex	412	378
Surrey	295	8
Suffolk	**93**	**13**
Herts	82	34
Hamps	80	0
Norfolk	**13**	**29**
Berks	12	1
Beds	10	3
Bucks	27	2
Cambs	-	1

+ More than 10 incidents   * All V2 incidents on land

V1 Incidents (land and sea)

Phase 1 13 June–1 Sept	Phase 2 5 Sept–14 Jan	Phase 3 3–29 March	Total
6,725	638	125	7,488

1054 V2 Incidents on land, plus 61 in sea. Total of 1115

Civilian Casualties in England

	V1	V2
Killed	6,184	2,754
Seriously injured	17,981	6,523

Source. Collier, B., *History of The Second World War, The Defence of the United Kingdom* (HMSO and Longmans, Green, 1957), Appendices XLV, XLVIII, XLIX, L.

Appendix VI

HAA Diver Gun Site Locations in Norfolk and Suffolk

24 November 1944

Site ref	OS Map ref.	Bty.	Regt.	Location	Notes
K1	TM325364	468	136	N of Felixstowe	
K22	TM319356	439 (Ind)		Felixstowe, Brackenbury Fort	
H1	TM286325	489	150	Landguard	GDA and Diver
H2	TM278360	489	150	Trimley	GDA and Diver
H4	TM243342	—		Shotley	
H12	TM203417	—		Nacton Heath	GDA. Diver?
H14	TM216442	—		Foxhall Heath	GDA. Diver?
H16	TM142402	—		W of Wherstead	GDA. Diver?
H18	TM164467	—		Grove Farm, N of Ipswich	GDA. Diver?
G1	TM435500	663 (Ind)		Orford Town marshes	

G2	TM422495	663 (Ind)		Chantry Marshes, Orford	
G3	TM407481	440 (Ind)		Gedgrave Marshes	
G4	TM401476	440 (Ind)		Gedgrave Marshes	
G5	TM392472	434 (Ind)		Boyton Marshes	
G6	TM387463	434 (Ind)		Boyton Marshes	
G7	TM358403	429	140	East Lane, Bawdsey	
G8	TM368436	420	140	Oxley Marshes	
G9	TM361433	429	140	Shingle Street	
G10	TM361428	430	140	Shingle Street	
G11	TM356413	430	140	E of Alderton	
G12	TM354406	420	140	E of Bawdsey	
G13	TM347388	418	140	NE of Bawdsey Manor	
G14	TM350391	418	140	NE of Bawdsey Manor	
G15	TM434503	V		Orford Town Marshes	
G16	TM406490	V		Gedgrave Hall	
S1	TM464619	433	127	Leiston, The Walks	
S2	TM473611	437	138	Ness House, Thorpeness	
S3	TM476604	437	138	Thorpeness Common	
S4	TM457603	438	138	S of Aldringham Common	
S5	TM460593	438	138	North Warren	
S6	TM450587	433	127	South Warren	
S7	TM460585	424	138	Gorse Hill, N of Aldeburgh	

S8	TM460577	424	138	N of Aldeburgh	
S9	TM439556	422	127	High Street, Iken	
S10	TM428546	419	138	NE of Sudbourne	
S11	TM433546	419	138	NE of Sudbourne	
S12	TM437529	422	127	Valley Farm, Sudbourne	
S13	TM432517	372	119	Sudbourne Marshes	
S14	TM432508	372	119	Raydon Hall, Orford	
S15	TM470620	450	135	E of Sizewell Hall	2 HAA site?
S16	TM446547	447	135	Ferry Farm, Sudbourne	
T1	TM474727	415	124	Foxburrow Wood	
T2	TM483729	415	124	Sandymount Covert	
T3	TM475711	400	122	Bridge Farm, Dunwich	
T4	TM476699	400	122	Greyfriars House, Dunwich	
T5	TM475673	412	124	Coney Hill, Minsmere	
T6	TM478679	412	124	Dunwich Heath	
T7	TM458634	397	122	Leiston Common	
T8	TM475650	397	122	Goose Hill, Leiston	
T9	TM521821	401	122	N Common Wood, Covehithe	
T10	TM521802	219	124	Easton Wood, Covehithe	
T11	TM516787	219	124	Easton Bavents	
T12	TM502763	401	122	Southwold Common	
T13	TM486748	410	124	Walberswick Common	
T14	TM461628	410	124	S of Leiston Common	

T15	TM473637	369	117	Sizewell	
T16	TM460680	369	117	Westleton Walks	
T17	TM519787	370	117	Easton Farm, Easton Bavents	
T18	TM451695	370	117	Westleton Heath	
T19	TM512806	TB1		Porter's Farm, South Cove	
T20	TM491742	TA1		Oldtown Marshes, Walberswick	
T21	TM463698	TA2		Westleton Heath	
T22	TM462650	TA3		Ash Wood, Westleton	
YH1	TG505114	518	139 (M)	West Caister	GDA and Diver
YH2	TG525025	484	139 (M)	S of Gorleston	GDA and Diver
YA	TM531837	512	149 (M)	Beach Farm, Benacre	
YB	TM535865	608	183 (M)	Kessingland	
YC	TM535877	506	149 (M)	Cliff Farm Cottage, Kessingland	
YD	TM538891	478	161 (M)	Pakefield Hall	
YE	TM555939	485	135 (M)	Lowestoft Ness	
YF	TM547961	579	172 (M)	Gunton	
YG	TM540982	484	139 (M)	Corton	
YH	TM532008	507	149 (M)	N E of Hopton	

The locations are nearby names for guidance to the position.

GDA=Gun Defended Area (pre Diver).

— Sites not mentioned in sources but known to have Diver role.

V=vacant. Site known to have Diver role.

(M)=Mixed male and females sites. There were other mixed sites.

(Ind)=Independent Battery.

* map ref. in War Diary is in the sea. Adjusted for likely position.

For data on other periods and LAA refer to reference below.

Source. Dobinson, C., *Operation Diver*, pp. 422 to 428.

Appendix VII

PHASE 2 OF V1 ATTACKS

5 SEPTEMBER 1944 TO 15 JANUARY 1945

Air-launched V1s over East Anglian coast (excludes Manchester raid)

Month	Approach coast *	Shot down over land AA	Shot down over land Fighters	Shot down over sea AA	Shot down over sea Fighters
Sept.	80	11	4	7	1
Oct.	203	45	25	58	14
Nov.	188	37	11	90	4
Dec.	86	15	7	43	0
Jan.	51	13	1	17	0
TOTAL	608	121	48	215	19

* Many of the V1s launched from the Heinkel aircraft aborted soon after. This column represents the number that approached the coast, to either be shot down over the sea or land, or continue on to their final point of impact.

The first incident in this Phase was on 16 September.

The figures in this table are derived from the following sources:

Collier, B., *History of the Second World War: The Defence of the United Kingdom* (HMSO and Longmans Green, 1957)

Hill, Sir Roderick, Supplement to *The London Gazette*, 19 October, 1948.

Ramsey, W., *The V-Weapons Then And Now* (Battle of Britain International, 2020)

Smith, P., *Air-launched Doodlebugs, The Forgotten Campaign* (Pen and Sword Aviation, 2006)

Appendix VIII

HAA Gun Site Activity

Aldeburgh, Thorpeness, Sudbourne and Orford

138 HAA Regiment, 5 Brigade
November and December 1944
Category A   V1 blown up
Category B   V1 damaged
V1s engaged by the 3.7- inch guns firing Bonzo proximity fused shells

Date	V1s	Cat A	Cat B	Bonzo fired	Site Location	Site/Battery
4 Nov.	1	1		16	Sudbourne	S10, S11, 419 Bty
	2	2		51	Aldeburgh	S7, S8, 424 Bty
	3	2	1	89	Thorpeness	S2, S3, 437 Bty
5 Nov.	1		1	3	Sudbourne	S10, 419 Bty
*	1		1	31	Aldeburgh	S7, 424 Bty
	1		1	23	Thorpeness	S3, 437 Bty
	2	2		55	Thorpeness/ Aldeburgh	S4, S5, 438 Bty
6 Nov.	4	3	1	39	Aldeburgh	424 Bty
	2	2		66	Thorpeness	S2, S3, 437 Bty
	4	3	1	94	Aldeburgh	438 Bty
8 Nov.	1		1	10	Aldeburgh	424 Bty
9 Nov.	1			20	Sudbourne	S11, 419 Bty
	2			27	Aldeburgh	424 Bty
	2	1		55	Thorpeness	S2, S3, 437 Bty
	2	1		79	Aldeburgh	438 Bty
10 Nov.	3	1		39	Sudbourne	S10, S11, 419 Bty
	6	2	2	127	Aldeburgh	424 Bty
	5	2	2	122	Thorpeness	S2, S3, 437 Bty
	5	3	1	284	Aldeburgh	438 Bty
11 Nov.	1		1	12	Sudbourne	S11, 419 Bty
	2		2	126	Thorpeness	S2, S3, 437 Bty

13 Nov.	2	1	1	106	Sudbourne	S11, 419 Bty
	1			9	Aldeburgh	424 Bty
	1		2	66	Thorpeness	S2, S3, 437 Bty
14 Nov.	1	1		45	Sudbourne	S10, S11, 419 Bty
	3	1	1	77	Aldeburgh	424 Bty
	2	1	1	89	Thorpeness	S2, S3, 437 Bty
	3	1	2	126	Aldeburgh	438 Bty
19 Nov.	1		1	60	Sudbourne	S10, S11, 419 Bty
	1		1	31	Aldeburgh	424 Bty
22 Nov.	2		2	43	Aldeburgh	424/438 Btys
23 Nov.	2		1	33	Sudbourne	S10, S11, 419 Bty
	2		2	47	Thorpeness	S2, 437 Bty
5 Dec.	1	1		20	Aldeburgh/ Thorpeness	S4, S5, 438 Bty
7 Dec.	1			30	Sudbourne	419 Bty
12 Dec.	3	2		25	Sudbourne	
13 Dec.	6	2	4	211	Aldeburgh/ Thorpeness	S2, S3, S4, S5, S7, S8
	3	1	2	84	Thorpeness	S2, S3, 437 Bty
18 Dec.	7	1	5	297	Sudbourne	S13, S14
	6	3		188	Aldeburgh	S7, S8
	3	3		116	Thorpeness	S2, S3
23 Dec.	2	2		79	Sudbourne/ Orford	S13, S14
TOTAL	104	45	40	3150		

The location refers to the nearest town or village. These site locations are shown on Fig. 6.2. For further details see Appendix VI.

The above snapshot of AA fire in the Diver Strip shows that for these locations, 82 per cent of the 104 V1s engaged in this period were either blown up or damaged, with an average expenditure of 37 rounds for each kill.

A site would typically consist of four 3.7-inch guns.

* The incident when a V1 struck the gun at S7 but did not explode.

The format of the data in the War Diaries is not consistent, and the above reflects the extent of the information provided for these sites.

Source. TNA, WO 166/1497, 138 HAA Regiment War Diary.

Appendix IX

REPORT OF AIR RAID ON 18TH OCTOBER, 1944

COUNTY BOROUGH OF IPSWICH

On Wednesday, 18th October, 1944, we received air raid warning "red" at 23.12 hours, Observer Corps alarm at 23.25, Observer Corps release at 23.44, and air raid message "white" at 23.46 hours.

Within two minutes of the Observer Corps alarm a "Fly Bomb" travelling approximately south-west from the East Coast fell and exploded on an Anderson shelter at the rear of No. 5, Halton Crescent in the Priory Heath housing estate just north of Ipswich Airport. The Anderson shelter was one of a pair covered by the same mound of earth, the neighbouring shelter being in the garden of No. 3, Halton Crescent. The Anderson shelter was destroyed and a shallow crater formed. The residents at No. 5 were not at home and the shelter was unoccupied. The shelter at No. 3, occupied by four people, was severely damaged, and the husband, wife and elder son of the Edwards family were killed and the younger son seriously injured. The husband and son were dead when taken from the shelter, and the wife was dead on arrival at hospital. A warden, Arthur John Last, was blown down the steps at the entrance to Wardens' Post No. 9 and is amongst the seriously injured.

A block of four houses, Nos. 3, 5, 7 and 9 Halton Crescent were totally demolished. Anderson shelters at Nos. 7 and 9, similarly placed under a single mound at the rear of the houses, were damaged, and a baby of two months was drawn by blast from the shelter at the rear of No. 7 on to the roadway. She died later.

Although preliminary reports gave damage to water, gas and electricity mains, the damage was confined to the carcase internal pipes. Fifteen other houses in Halton Crescent and Campbell Road were seriously damaged, while blast damage to tiles, windows, doors etc., extended north-east to practically every house to Cody Road and Cranwell Crescent with occasional damage on Felixstowe Road; to the north-west to Priory Heath Schools; to the south-west to houses on Nacton Road from Maryon Road almost to the airport buildings; and to the south-east to four industrial premises - Messrs: Adlard's, West's, Wrinch's and Crane's. Damage conformed to limits previously given - i.e. (a) 75 feet; (b) 120 feet; (c) and (d) ½ mile.

The fall of the Fly was promptly reported and two rescue squads and four ambulances were despatched immediately. Two complete crews of the N.F.S. [National Fire Service] were also quickly on the scene and rendered considerable aid to the rescue squads. The N.F.S. removed coal fires that had been left burning in about twelve damaged houses. A mobile canteen and other services were quickly built up and a plus of all services was experienced. Approximately thirty wardens from a neighbouring Group helped in a house-to-house search for other casualties. At the end of the operational period a very useful service was performed by searchlight units stationed in the County area on this side of the Borough by laying searchlights over the damaged district. These were maintained until given information that all work had been completed. It was a very dark night and this extra lighting was greatly appreciated.

Casualty Bureau Return gives:

1 male, 1 female and 2 children dead.

3 males, 4 females and 1 child injured and detained.

5 males and 6 females injured-other cases.

The Borough Engineer's survey gives:

Dwelling Houses totally destroyed - 4.

Dwelling houses so badly damaged that demolition is necessary - 4.

Dwelling houses seriously damaged but capable of repair

   (a) still usable — 11
   (b) evacuated or to be evacuated — 33

Slightly damaged — 340 dwelling houses, 4 industrial establishments, 1 public building and 1 other property.

First aid repairs were commenced at daylight, and are now completed over the larger part of the area. Extended work has now commenced. Practically all the dwelling properties are in the ownership of the Ipswich Corporation. Damage to Messrs. Crane's factory was to glass and asbestos corrugated sheets and did not delay production.

Holywells Rest centre was opened at 23.50 hours on the 18th and 63 persons were admitted. The Centre remained open throughout the following day and 79 persons were accommodated on the night of the 29th October. The Centre had to be open on the 29th because it was impossible to rehouse the large families involved in the short time. The Centre closed at 17.00 hours on the 29th October.

Billeting Officers operating from the Rest Centre and an Incident Enquiry Point billeted a total of 107 people (70 adults and 37 children), the great majority of these being accommodated with relatives or friends. A total of 15 families were rehoused.

An Incident Enquiry Point was set up at 26, Campbell Road at 08.00 hours on the 19th and remained open until 19.00 hours the same day, re-opening at 05.00 hours on the 20th, and finally closing at 18.30 hours. They were categorised as follows:-

Relatives and friends	17
Accommodation and billets	41
Rations	14
Clothing	2
Transport of furniture	19
Miscellaneous	29

The Point served a useful purpose and seemed to be appreciated by the people. On the following day, the 19th, 69 persons, and on the 20th 36 persons, from the damaged area, were given dinner at the British Restaurant situated a short distance from the damaged site at the labour Club, Landseer Road. This covered the period when they without normal cooking facilities.

All casualties and serious damage were in East Suffolk County Council area, but by arrangement the area is policed and covered by Civil Defence from the borough of Ipswich, owing to the peculiar boundary line which at present runs diagonally through the Corporation housing estate.

Morale was maintained. A mobile canteen of the Salvation Army provided acceptable assistance to canteens of the borough. This aid (commencing in 1940 with tea urns on a perambulator) has been associated with most bombing that has taken place.

(Signed) C. J. Cresswell
Chief Constable.
A.R.P. Controller
Town Hall,
Ipswich.
28th October, 1944.

Source. Suffolk Archives reference HD 862

Glossary

AA	Anti-Aircraft
ADGB	Air Defence of Great Britain
ALD	Air-Launched Doodlebug
ARP	Air Raid Precautions
ATS	Auxiliary Territorial Service. Women's branch of Army
Bonzo	Proximity fuse fitted to shells
Bty	Battery
CH	Chain Home
CHEL	Chain Home Extra Low
CHL	Chain Home Low
FIDO	Fog Investigation and Dispersal Operation
GCI	Ground Controlled Interception radar
GDA	Gun Defended Area
HAA	Heavy Anti-Aircraft
Heer	German Army
IFF	Identify Friend or Foe
LAA	Light Anti-Aircraft
Luftwaffe	Aerial warfare branch of the German Wehrmacht
ORB	Operations Record Books
PPI	Plan Position Indicator
PRU	Photo Reconnaissance Unit
Radar	Radio direction and ranging
RAF	Royal Air Force
RDC	Rural District Council
RDF	Radio Direction Finding
Regt	Regiment
REME	Royal Electrical and Mechanical Engineers
RN	Royal Navy
ROC	Royal Observer Corps
Tallboy	12,000 lb bomb designed by Barnes Wallis
USAAF	United States Army Air Force
UXB	Unexploded Bomb
WAAF	Women's Auxiliary Air Force

Select Bibliography

Banger, Joan   *Norwich at War* (Poppyland Publishing, 2003)

Bowyer, Michael   *Air Raid, The enemy air offensive against East Anglia 1939–1945* (Patrick Stephens, 1986)

Cabell, Craig and Thomas, Graham

                        Operation Big Ben, The anti-V2 Spitfire missions 1944–1945 (Spellmount, 2004)

Campbell, Christy   *Target London, under attack from the V-weapons during WW11* (Abacus, 2013)

Collier, Basil   *The Battle of the V-Weapons 1944–1945* (Hodder and Stoughton, 1964)

                        The Defence of the United Kingdom (HMSO and Longmans, Green, 1957)

Dobinson, Colin   *Operation Diver* (Historic England, 2019)

Douglas Brown, R.   *East Anglia 1944 and 1945* (The Lavenham Press, 1992 and 1994)

Freeman, Roger   *The Mighty Eighth, a History of the U.S. Army Air Force* (Macdonald and Jane's, 1978)

Greehan, John   *Hitler's V-Weapons, The Battle Against The V-1 & V-2, Written At The Time* (Frontline Books, 2020)

Heath, David   *Shout and Whisper* (Bawdsey Radar Trust, 2010)

Hogg, Ian   *German Secret Weapons of the Second World War* (Frontline Books, 2015)

Jennings, Mick, MBE   *Royal Air Force Coltishall Fighter Station, A Station History* (Old Forge Publishing, 2007)

Jones, David   *Ipswich in the Second World War* (Phillimore, 2005)

Jones, R.V.   *Most Secret War, British Scientific Intelligence 1939–1945* (Book Club Associates, 1978)

Kinsey, Gordon   *Bawdsey, Birth of the Beam* (Terence Dalton, 1983)

                        Orfordness Secret Site (Terence Dalton, 1981)

Latham, Colin and Stobbs, Ann

                        The Birth of British Radar, The memoirs of Arnold 'Skip' Wilkins (Radio Society of Great Britain, 2011)

Liddiard, Robert and Sims, David

                        A Very Dangerous Locality, The landscape of the Suffolk

	Sandlings in the Second World War (University of Hertfordshire Press, 2018)
Meeres, Frank	*Norfolk in the Second World War* (Phillimore, 2006)
O'Brien, T. H.	*History of the Second World War; Civil Defence* (HMSO and Longmans, Green, 1955)
Ogley, Bob	*Doodlebugs and Rockets, The Battle of the Flying Bombs* (Froglets Publications, 1992)
Olsen, Jack	*Aphrodite, Desperate Mission* (New York, Putnam, 1970)
Ramsey, Winston (ed.)	*The V-Weapons Then And Now* (Battle of Britain International, 2020)
Routledge, N. W., Brigadier, OBE, TD	
	Anti-Aircraft Artillery 1914–55 (Brassey's, 1994)
Smith, Graham	*Norfolk Airfields in the Second World War* (Countryside Books, 1997)
	Suffolk Airfields in the Second World War (Countryside Books, 1995)
Smith, Peter	*Air-Launched Doodlebugs, The Forgotten Campaign* (Pen and Sword Aviation, 2006)
Wood, Derek	*Attack Warning Red, The Royal Observer Corps and the Defence of Britain, 1925 to 1975* (Macdonald and Jane's, 1976)
Young, Richard Anthony	*The Flying Bomb* (Sky Books Press, 1978)
Zaloga, Steven	*German V-Weapon Sites 1943-1945* (Osprey Publishing, 2008)
	Operation Crossbow 1944, Hunting Hitler's V-Weapons (Osprey Publishing, 2018)

Index